RAYMOND A. MOOT

M.A. and Ph.D. from the University of Virginia. After teaching philosophy at East Carolina University, he received his M.D. from the Medical College of Georgia in 1976 and then served his residency at the University of Virginia Medical School. He is a bestselling author whose works include *Life After Life*, *The Light Beyond* and *Life After Loss*.

Paul Perry, co-author of *The Light Beyond* and *Transformed by the Light*, lives in Arizona.

"Moody's here to offer another breakthrough . . . The book is filled with historical and literary accounts of visionary experiences, proving that the desire to contact the departed is as old as life itself." – *Booklist*

"Skeptics should remember that near-death experiences had no scientific standing before Moody's research established the phenomenon as a legitimate field of inquiry . . . Now, [in *Reunited*], Moody offers instructions on how to contact the dead." – *Publishers Weekly*

"Detailed instructions on how to communicate with the dead highlight the sequel to *Life After Life*, which offers clear evidence for the existence of life after death and a collection of accounts of the paranormal." – *Book Alert*

REUNITED

How to Meet Loved Ones Again Who Seem Lost to Death

Raymond Moody

with Paul Perry

RIDER

LONDON • SYDNEY • AUCKLAND • JOHANNESBURG

5 7 9 10 8 6 4

First published as *Reunions* in the United States in 1993 by
The Ballantine Publishing Group

This revised and updated edition first published in the UK in 2006 by Rider,
an imprint of Ebury Publishing, Random House,
20 Vauxhall Bridge Road, London SW1V 2SA

Addresses for companies within the Random House Group
Limited can be found at:
www.randomhouse.co.uk/offices.htm

The Random House Group Limited Reg. No. 954009

Penguin Random House is committed to a sustainable future for
our business, our readers and our planet. This book is made from
Forest Stewardship Council® certified paper.

MIX
Paper from
responsible sources
FSC® C018179

Printed and bound in Great Britain by Clays Ltd, Elcograf S.p.A.

A CIP catalogue record for this book
is available from the British Library

ISBN 9781846040481

Grateful acknowledgement is made for permission to reprint excerpts from the
following: *Asclepius, Volume I* by Emma J. and Ludwig Edelstein (reprinted by
permission of Ayer Company Publishers Inc.); *The Paranormal and the Normal* by
Morton Leeds and Gardner Murphy (reprinted by permission of Scarecrow Press,
Inc.); *Plants of the Gods* by Richard Evans Schultes and Albert Hoffman (reprinted
by permission of the Healing Arts Press, an imprint of Inner Traditions
International); *A Study of History, Volume X* by Arnold Toynbee (reprinted by
permission of Oxford University Press)

CONTENTS

PREFACE

It is in the nature of human beings to wonder whether there is an afterlife. And millions of people everywhere long to be reunited with loved ones lost to death. Therefore, it is strange that the astonishing history of the ancient Greek oracles of the dead is not a matter of common knowledge. This book attempts to rectify that situation by resurrecting simple time-honored techniques for evoking the spirits of the departed. In these pages, you will learn an effective procedure for envisioning deceased people, for feeling their presence, hearing their voices, conversing with them, and healing your grief.

Of course, these claims may appear too outrageous to be believed, too bizarre even for tabloid journalism. The true story of the oracles of the dead is perhaps too sensational for sensationalism itself to embrace. So, it is best to begin by explaining the role evocation of the spirits of the dead played in the origins of Western thought.

Early Greek philosophers like Pythagoras, Heraclitus and Plato introduced the topic of life after death as a subject for rational inquiry. In fact, the mystery of an afterlife was one of the original questions upon which they founded the Western philosophical and scientific tradition. Ordinary Greeks believed that a philosopher was someone who "meddles in things under the earth." This phrase was also a euphemism for the rites for raising ghosts that were practiced at oracles of the dead by technicians known as psychogogues. Plainly, their contemporaries thought of philosophers as psychogogues, and the popular perception that Plato's mentor Socrates evoked the dead was factored into his trial and execution. It is unclear whether Socrates himself actually ever participated in such activities, but certain other philosophers plainly did. Empedocles, for example – the great philosopher who first propounded a theory of evolution – was associated with evocation of the deceased as it was practiced on the slopes of Mt. Etna in Sicily. Later on, Plato himself alluded to the practice of evoking the dead and acknowledged the historical tradition linking philosophy to death. He characterized philosophy as a kind of rehearsal for dying, and noted that, in seeking to know the truth, philosophers are always trying to escape the limitations of their physical bodies.

The Greek oracles of the dead thrived for at least a thousand years. During that time, these outlandish, subterranean institutions made their mark not only on philosophy but on Western literature as well. A constant stream of desperate people made their way to remote, desolate spots hoping to get a glimpse of a beloved Aunt Melissa or a trusted Uncle Aristocles. And when the pilgrims arrived at an oracle of the dead, the resident psychogogues' sophisticated technology and inherited know-how virtually guaranteed that the seekers would undergo profound, life-changing experiences. It is not surprising that touching tales of visionary reunions with the deceased should find their way into Greek literature and hence, through the millennia, into today's popular movies.

The enduring tale of the magical musician Orpheus is the best-known story to derive from an encounter at an oracle of the dead. His music tamed wild animals and even made trees bow down, but Orpheus fell into a deep despondency when his true love Eurydice died. Unable to cope, he traveled to an oracle of the dead, perhaps the famous one on the Acheron River in Thesprotia, in the far, northwestern corner of Greece, which I describe in this book. He played his lyre to summon an apparition of Eurydice but, because he muffed the instructions, he failed to lead her out of the underworld.

Even after the oracles of the dead had become long-forgotten, writers continued to pass along this enchanting tale. It persists today, told and retold in a plethora of movie versions, including *A Portrait of Jenny* with Joseph Cotton, Anthony Minghella's *Truly Madly Deeply*, James Cameron's *Titanic*, and Robin Williams's *What Dreams May Come*. The degree to which the story of Orpheus' other-world adventure has penetrated popular culture proves that evocation of the deceased is part of the collective cultural heritage of humankind.

It follows that, by learning how, in Shakespeare's words, to "call spirits from the vasty deep," we are reconnecting with our intellectual and historical roots in a very real way. In the process, we stand to recover an important lost art for alleviating grief, the source of life's worst miseries.

In the years since this book was first published in 1993, I have guided hundreds of individuals through vivid apparitional encounters with departed friends and relatives, and taught the procedure to a couple of hundred physicians, psychologists, and psychotherapists. Some of them have replicated my findings and reported on their work in scholarly journals. For example, Arthur Hastings, a respected professor at the Institute of Transpersonal Psychology in California, conducted a study using the procedure and apparatus I designed, which, in my research, facilitated dramatic visitations on their first attempts in fifty percent of the subjects who participated. Subsequently, the Institute incorporated evocation of the deceased into their curriculum, and today it is taught to psychotherapists-in-training. Of course, we do not yet understand this procedure well enough to consider it a reliable therapy for grief. Even so, early results are promising, and given that so many investigators are working with the technique, knowledge in this area is sure to expand, albeit gradually.

Will these developments bring us closer to a rational solution of the deepest mystery of human existence? Frankly, it depends on whether we are willing to take the question seriously, and own up to the enormous difficulties that the ancient Greek philosophers propounded. In this age of sound-bites, of instant gratification, quick fixes, and over-reliance on scientific solutions, few have the patience to think carefully and rationally about a question of this magnitude. Unfortunately, some investigators are happy to participate in society's self-delusions, and occasionally announce that their experiments provide "scientific evidence" of an afterlife. I have always eschewed that label, "scientific." In my opinion, the proper scientific attitude towards life after death is to acknowledge that it is not yet a scientific question. Still, we ought to grant that it is an important question, perhaps the most important question we can ask. And we ought to keep whittling away at it, trying any rational approach that makes sense, while scrupulously avoiding scientism, the false doctrine that scientific method is the only rational means of finding out the truth, and of establishing knowledge. Philosophy, with its long tradition of careful, logical reasoning and conceptual analysis, is far more likely to yield a breakthrough in this field than science is.

Plato's wise advice on the issue is about the best that anyone has ever given. As he pointed out in his dialogue *Phaedo*, in the present life it is exceedingly difficult, and probably impossible, to attain any sort of certainty about questions concerning an afterlife. Still, a person would really have to be a lazy, shiftless sort not to give it his or her best shot. We should put every theory we can find or dream up to the most rigorous and rational tests we can conceive. And we ought not to relent until we have looked at every theory from every possible angle, and exhausted every resource of our rational intelligence. We are obliged to proceed in one of two ways. Either we must find out what the facts are, by seeking instruction or by discerning them for ourselves. Or, if that proves impossible, we ought to choose the most plausible and reliable theory humans can devise, and use it as a raft to ride the seas of life. And, even then, of course, a direct revelation from God would be a far surer means of guiding life's journey.

Truly, given its centrality in Greek philosophy and the emotional vulnerability of those who are grieving or who are fearful of death, we owe the question of life after death a respect that borders on veneration. In my view, it is a kind of sin to approach this great mystery with slapdash logic in hasty attempts to prove life after death. In many cases, the objective of scholars who commit this sin is to make people feel better. This is not solely the fault of individual investigations, however, for it is inherent in the Western intellectual tradition.

Ancient philosophers saw consolation as a legitimate purpose of rational inquiry. They figured that if they could come up with strong, rational arguments in favor of life after death, it would console the grieving and cheer up elderly or terminally ill people who were afraid of death. Philosophers of every school published books that compiled arguments that might offer their readers hope and consolation as they faced the reality of death. But the consolation of grieving people is no excuse for helping them to deceive themselves, and the best, most effective, consolation is the truth.

In that regard, I believe that there are good reasons to

be hopeful. I believe that the twenty-first century will see solid, measurable progress toward a rational under-standing of this immense, deep mystery. Specifically, I believe that major advances are right around the corner, and that they will be conceptual breakthroughs – not scientific ones. Although I no longer operate a research facility for evoking the deceased, other investigators are forging ahead with this work, and I continue to pursue other related lines of inquiry.

In the near future, I hope to publish a book that genuinely advances the debate by working out an alter-nate logic, or a set of rational principles. This will open promising new advances for research. I plan a vast, collective experiment that will actually reshape the rational mind to enable people to think more clearly and cogently about the fate of the soul at death. Concurrently, tens of millions of men and women who were born soon after World War II are waking up to their own mortality, and to that of their loved ones. Enormous, demographic forces are generating a tidal wave of serious interest in the prospect of our conscious existence in a world beyond death. We ought to be prepared for some truly mind-boggling developments that will dramatically change the landscape of the controversy.

Dr. Raymond Moody

INTRODUCTION

One of the greatest pains to human nature is the pain of a new idea.

—Walter Bagetiot

The wish for reunion with loved ones lost to death is among the most poignant and insistent of human desires. The desire taunts and saddens us with a litany of *what ifs* and *if onlys*, and mournful pleas for only five minutes more.

Sometimes this wish is fulfilled in the form of visions or apparitions of the deceased, experiences reportedly quite distinct from dreams. These are waking interludes during which the living presence of the deceased person is vividly and—it seems—unmistakably felt or sensed. These episodes are typically convincing, even self-certifying in that a person who undergoes them may have no doubt that the encounter was real and is consequently left with the conviction that there is indeed life beyond death.

The universal experience of apparitions has found its way into the language and folklore of cultures all over the world, from a time long before the beginning of recorded history. Even today visionary reunions with the departed are remarkably common. A number of studies published in medical journals and other scholarly sources have established that a high percentage of bereaved persons have visions of the deceased. Studies suggest that as many as 66 percent of widows experience apparitions of their departed husbands.

Widows have been selected as the subject of these investigations for the simple reason that women tend to outlive men. There are more widows, making them more accessible for study. Clinical experience reveals that apparitions of the deceased are common among other bereaved groups too—children, parents, siblings, and friends of the deceased. For instance, as many as 75 percent of parents who lose a child to death will have some kind of apparition of that child within a year of the loss. This experience is a relief for most of the parents and will greatly reduce their grief.

A form of apparition is common among people who have near-death experiences too. They tell us that as they enter into a realm of light, they are met by the spirits of relatives and friends who have previously died. These experiences are often transformative, frequently having positive after effects.

If one could replicate the near-death experience and bring it about in people of good health, then it seemed possible that those powerful after effects could be used in grief therapy. The appeal of this idea is shown by its success as a theme in various Hollywood movies.

Still I remained interested in duplicating the near-death experience, especially that portion in which the person sees departed loved ones. Although seeing departed loved ones represented only one component of these experiences, I felt that by facilitating apparitions, I might learn about the near-death experience as a whole. Still, I didn't know how to do that.

Then one day the answer fell on me—literally.

It happened on an autumn day in 1987. I was browsing through the shelves of a used-book store in a small Georgia town. As I walked toward a section of art books in the back of the store, a book fell off the shelves and dropped at my feet.

Bending over to pick it up, I noticed that its title was *Crystal Gazing*. My initial sensation was one of disgust. Mirror gazing (which is a more appropriate term for this practice) has always been associated with fraud and deceit—the Gypsy woman bilking clients or the fortune-teller who needs more money before he can clearly see the visions in the crystal ball. I would have put the book back on the shelf at that point had I not remembered a conversation I had had with Dr. William Roll, a pioneer in the study of the paranormal, who said that people did indeed see visions in the clear depth of mirrors. Out of curiosity I flipped through a few pages and then began reading the first chapter. The author, Northcote Thomas, was a compulsive and serious scholar. He discussed some of the methods of mirror gazing and briefly covered elements of its psychology.

Perhaps the most interesting part of the book was the introduction from Andrew Lang, an eminent scholar. He expressed the belief that the psychological and scientific community would be appalled by anyone who dared attempt a rational examination of mirror gazing. He was quick to point out that such a reaction would be unfair, since it would keep inquisitive people from examining the mysteries of the mind. He sought to quell the fears that might arise among those in the medical and scientific profession. As he wrote:

> In merely examining mirror gazing we are on the border of the realm of quackery, fraud, blind credulity, avid hopes, and superstitious fears. There is no doubt at all that, this border once crossed, even minds practised in the physical sciences often cease to be scientific or sensible . . . Thus we can explain the aversion of men of science to the examination of phenomena—no more offensive, really, than the dreams of the day or the night. They are phenomena of human nature, exercises of human faculty, and, as such, invite study. To shirk examination is less than courageous.

Through the book I became excited at the possibilities of mirror gazing. I had been studying some of the ways in which cultures had created and used altered states of consciousness. In the course of this work I had stumbled upon a number of accounts in which apparitions of the dead were evoked among living people. Most notable were the experiences in the Greek oracles of the dead, or *psychomanteums*, where people journeyed to consult with spirits of the deceased. Accounts that have survived from those remote times make it clear that people actually seemed to see and be in direct contact with the departed during those visits.

This book and the additional research made me realize that visions of departed loved ones were far more accessible than had previously been believed. I began to consider a number of questions that mirror gazing might answer:

Does this explain why so many people see ghosts? The seeing of ghosts or apparitions is an extremely common phenomenon. Some very well-done studies have shown that as many as one fourth of Americans will admit to having seen a ghost at least once, compared with one third of some Europeans.

People who experience apparitions not only see the dead, but may also hear, feel, and sometimes even smell them. All of these encounters are powerful reminders that those we love are deeply embedded in our unconscious mind. So deeply embedded in fact that it is not a great leap to think that we should not continue to communicate with them in one form or another.

Carl Sagan, the Cornell University astronomer and author, wrote about his own experience in *Parade* magazine: "Probably a dozen times since their deaths I've heard my mother or father, in an ordinary, conversational tone of voice, call my name. They had called my name often during my life with them. I still miss them so much that it doesn't seem strange to me that my brain occasionally will retrieve a kind of lucid recollection of their voices."

It doesn't surprise me either. Although the physical body is gone, the spirit of the dead continues to occupy a vivid and important part of the mind. To be with them, maybe all we really need to do is figure out a way to delve into our unconscious minds. I thought that mirror gazing might be that way.

Can mirror gazing make it possible to study the seeing of "ghosts" in a laboratory setting? As I have pointed out, millions of people report having seen departed loved ones spontaneously, without trying to do so. These apparitions seemingly just happen on their own, without people working themselves into an appropriate mood.

Because of their spontaneous nature, the study of apparitional sightings is largely the study of stories, tales told by people who see ghosts and volunteer their accounts to researchers.

In the past, apparitions could not be made to happen, let alone be induced in a laboratory setting. The only method of study was to collect ghost stories from people and examine their similarities, which represented a true frustration for psychologists,

I began to wonder, could mirror gazing allow apparitions to be created in a controlled setting, where scientists could actually watch a person seeing a ghost? It was an exciting notion, to be sure.

Can reunions with departed loved ones be used in helping people overcome grief? Since grief is one of the most difficult of human emotions to overcome, I was particularly interested in this question. Maybe by mirror gazing, people could have an apparition of their late loved ones. Such an apparition might salve their grief.

As I stood in that dusty bookstore, I felt a stirring of excitement, knowing that my next few years would be spent exploring a field with great and untapped promise. With some sincere work and an open-minded approach, I felt certain I could bring mirror gazing from "the border of the realm of quackery," as Lang put it, and make it an accessible and valuable area of psychology.

I decided to spend some time in sincere study of this forgotten art. I went through the shelves of libraries in search of historical and literary references to mirror gazing.

I also decided to conduct an informal study in which I took a number of people through the process of mirror gazing. The results were so unexpected that I began to conduct mirror-gazing sessions as rapidly as I could, just to amass as many case studies as possible. From all of these gazing sessions I have concluded that mirror gazing can be used as:

First-person access to a truly fascinating but little-known dimension of our mental lives Much of what goes on in the human mind takes place in the unconscious. It is possible that mirror gazing makes the realm of the unconscious accessible and in a sense *visible*.

A tool that can be used by psychologists and psychiatrists to understand the inner worlds of their patients There are especially great possibilities in diagnosing mental and emotional difficulties and possibly, although this is a more dubious claim, in diagnosing physical illnesses as, well.

An educational tool for psychology instructors to explore the wonders of the human mind One should not dismiss the role of fun in education, nor in therapy for that matter. The fun of mirror gazing can awaken the latent interests of students.

A means of tapping creative abilities Writers, scientists, business people, and others have been able to use the trance state required for mirror gazing to overcome blocks to their creativity. I will give several examples of the creative use of techniques similar to mirror gazing by Thomas Edison, Charles Dickens, René Descartes, and others later in the book.

A key to understanding several perplexing incidents in history A study of mirror gazing also sheds light on the world of the ancients, who often made important decisions by consulting spirits of their relatives in the clear depth. The history chapter reveals many uses of mirror gazing through history. In recent years other historians have contacted me with similar accounts that are not included here. These incidents are sometimes hard to spot at first reading. I think this is true because mirror gazing was so common among the ancients that they didn't always describe it in their writings. It would be considered as unnecessary as, say, a modern writer describing how to make a telephone call.

If you are a history buff, mirror gazing will likely shed new light on old mysteries. It is especially valuable in understanding the world of prophets and visionaries who have guided civilizations for hundreds of years.

A way of exploring humankind's propensity to believe in occult beings and supernatural forces By understanding mirror gazing, the world of the paranormal can not only be studied but be re-created in a controlled laboratory setting as well.

Such a claim has never been made before. Indeed the problem science has with paranormal events, especially the seeing of apparitions, is that scientists have not been able to make apparitions happen in a laboratory. If a phenomenon can't be reproduced in a lab, science cannot study it effectively. In addition, if a phenomenon cannot be reproduced, science will often dismiss it as fraud.

Without arguing for or against the validity of such thought, let me just point out that mirror gazing allows people to see the spirits of departed relatives *virtually anytime they want*. Which means, of course, that the experience can be studied in a laboratory setting. For the first time, scientists can watch as someone "sees" a ghost. No longer will scientists have to wait for the experience to happen spontaneously and then attempt to study the event afterward.

The ability to see apparitions of departed relatives is probably the greatest benefit of all. For some people grief knows no bounds when they lose a loved one. Mirror gazing allows the bereaved to work out aspects of their grief. For me this is the most rewarding property of mirror gazing, since grief is one of the greatest psychological pains of all.

PARANORMAL POSSIBILITIES

If you are a reader of paranormal books, as I am, you surely pause from time to time as you read them and wonder. "Why haven't I had an experience like this?" I present to you yet another book on the paranormal, but this is one with a difference. By using the techniques described here, a considerable number of you will actually be able to experience visionary reunions with loved ones who are lost to death. First I recommend that anyone who seeks a visionary reunion by this method study the book in its entirety so as to achieve a thorough understanding of the process.

I also want to emphasize that this work has nothing to do with mediumship or séances. Mediums claim to possess some extraordinary capacity that enables them to contact the spirits of the dead on behalf of their clients and to convey messages back and forth. The client must accept that such a talent exists and that the particular medium possesses it. Mediumship provides at best a secondhand encounter. Indeed the word *medium* implies that communication is taking place through a third party.

The procedure described in this book works differently in that it enables subjects to have their own first-hand encounters with apparitions and to make their own assessments of the reality of the experience.

As human beings we are plagued by anxieties. There is one anxiety that we never overcome, and that is our fear of death. Fear of death is our greatest personal anxiety. It is the boundary we can never get past.

As a society we are very comfortable putting death in its place. We have created cemeteries in such a way that we keep death out of view. We have horror films to remind us of the terror of death. And we don't talk about death much in general, except when it is absolutely required.

All of these strictures are aimed at telling us that there is a world of the living and a world of the dead and that those on one side can never venture into the other. Period.

Yet in my experience there is a midway zone between these two lands. From a logical point of view this area has nothing in it. It is simply the zone between living and dying.

What cannot be doubted is that there are certain phenomena of living consciousness that seem to indicate that we survive death. Among those are near-death experiences, apparitions of the deceased, and shamanic voyages into the spirit world. These experiences are perceived as transitions between life and death, and they somehow have to do with both and yet with neither. In short they define what might be called the *Middle Realm*.

The existence of this Middle Realm defies scientific proof. And yet it is true that a significant proportion of people of sound mind and sensitive judgment undergo experiences that convince them that what we call death is merely a transition into another dimension of awareness, one called *life after death.*

With that in mind, mirror visions can certainly be included in those ways of entering the Middle Realm, and doing so safely.

Now I will recount for you what has become the adventure of a lifetime for me. I have conducted many people through these vivid visionary encounters, called *facilitated apparitions.* They have seen their departed loved ones, had conversations with them, and realized mysteries of the Middle Realm that they had only read about before. I, too, have had such an apparition. I conversed with my deceased grandmother, who appeared to be just as real as anyone could be. I have also discovered new meaning in some of the classics of literature and scholarship and have journeyed into uncanny ancient structures two thousand years old, which were designed to bring people in touch with their dead relatives. What follows is an intriguing mystery.

ONE

THE NATURE OF VISIONS

I sometimes define fantasy as something that I have been told by somebody else that I never saw myself.
—Michael Harner

Buried deep in the scientific literature are several studies that examine reunions with the departed.

The first such study that I am aware of was a "Census of Hallucinations," conducted in 1894. This fascinating work, led by Henry Sidgwick, a member of the Society for Psychical Research in England, asked seventeen thousand people the following deeply personal question: "Have you ever, when believing yourself to be completely awake; had a vivid impression of seeing or being touched by a living being or inanimate object, or of hearing a voice; which impression, as far as you could discover, was not due to any external physical cause?"

A "yes" answer led to a face-to-face interview with one of the 410 volunteers working on the study. More than 2,000 people answered in the affirmative. When obvious dreams and delirium were ruled out, the number of people who actually had apparitional visions was 1,684.

These accounts of encounters were benign and short in duration, usually lasting less than a minute. Many of the apparitions were seen in a medium similar to a mirror. Following is an example from a "Mrs. W.," which was recorded in 1885. In this experience she discusses seeing the upper half of a man with "a very pale face and dark hair and moustache" in the reflection of a window:

> One evening about 8:30, I had occasion to go into the drawingroom to get something out of the cupboard, when, on turning round, I saw the same face in the bay-window, in front of the shutters, which were closed. I again saw only the upper part of the figure, which seemed to be in a somewhat crouching posture. The light on this occasion came from the hall and the dining-room, and did not shine directly on the window; but I was able perfectly to distinguish the face and the expression of the eyes . . . On each of these occasions I was 8 to 10 feet distant from the figure.

The people who collected these experiences were unable to explain them. They did have theories, however. One was that a deceased person had left something behind in a certain locality and whatever was left communicates in some way with the living. Another speculation was that these apparitional sightings were hallucinations of the sane, vivid creations of the mind.

Whatever the case, the Society for Psychical Research concluded that there was no clear evidence for a 'post-mortem agency.'

The researchers claimed to have no other choice but to call the apparitional sighting 'hallucinations,' since they left no physical trace. They didn't deal with the possibility that Andrew Lang put forth later: "[Some] hallucinations are casual and unsought," he wrote in *Dreams and Ghosts.* "But between these and the dreams of sleep there is a kind of waking hallucination which some people can purposely evoke. Such are the visions of [mirror] gazing."

THE VISIONARY EXPERIENCE

The powerful and vivid quality of apparitions made me think they fit into the category of paranormal experience known as visions. Saint Paul's vision of Christ on the road to Damascus is one such example, as are the voices of angels that Joan of Arc heard that eventually led her to the command of the French army.

These occurrences are called *spontaneous* visions, which means people experience a vision without conscious effort. One moment everything seems normal, and the next moment a vision occurs.

A surprising number of spontaneous apparitions of the deceased are seen in mirrors or other reflective surfaces. Many others are seen in the night or against backgrounds such as a blank wall or in the dark outdoors.

For example, a woman told me that she had seen an apparition of her grandmother emerge from a mirror at the end of a hallway. As the amazed woman watched, the apparition walked down the hallway toward her, then vanished through an open doorway to another room. Another woman told me that she happened to look up at a crystal chandelier in her dining room and saw people talking to one another in one of the hanging crystals.

These visions have occurred throughout history to a variety of people. Abraham Lincoln, for instance, saw a double image of himself in a mirror at his home in Springfield, Illinois—one image as he was lying on a couch; the other looking ghostly and pale, like a dead or dying person.

What amazes me is not the visions President Lincoln had but the fact that he was willing to talk about them. For a president of the United States to talk about such an experience today would surely doom his political career, but Lincoln spoke freely about his dreams and visions.

Anatole France tells how his great-aunt saw a mirror vision of Robespierre dying at approximately the same time he was shot in the jaw. On the night of July 27, 1794, she was looking in a mirror when she shouted, "I see him! I see him! How pale he is! Blood is flowing from his mouth! His teeth and jaws are shattered! God be praised. The bloodthirsty wretch will drink no more blood but his own." Then she cried out and fainted.

On occasion collective mirror visions of the deceased have been reported. Most of the best documentation of these cases has come from researchers into the paranormal who are meticulous in their fact gathering.

One such investigator was Sir Ernest Bennett, the first

secretary of the Society for Psychical Research in England. He was intrigued by the unexplainable nature of many paranormal phenomena, especially those that happen spontaneously. He wrote extensively about the paranormal for scientific journals and carefully documented case studies of paranormal events. Among his case studies were examples of collective visions, ones in which more than one person sees an apparition of the same person at the same time. Following is one of his case studies that involves a surface similar to a mirror:

December 3rd, 1885

On the 5th April 1875 my wife's father, Captain Towns, died at his residence, Crankbrook, Rose Bay, near Sydney, N.S. Wales.

About six weeks after his death, my wife had occasion one evening about 9 o'clock, to go to one of the bedrooms in the house. She was accompanied by a young lady, Miss Berthon, and as they entered the room—the gas was burning all the time—they were amazed to see, reflected as it were on the polished surface of the wardrobe, the image of Captain Towns. It was barely half figure—the head, shoulders, and part of the arms only showing—in fact, it was like an ordinary medallion portrait, but life-size. The face appeared wan and pale, as it did before his death; and he wore a kind of grey flannel jacket, in which he had been accustomed to sleep. Surprised and half alarmed at what they saw, their first idea was that a portrait had been hung in the room and that what they saw was its reflection—but there was no picture of the kind.

Whilst they were looking and wondering, my wife's sister, Miss Towns, came into the room and before either of the others had time to speak she exclaimed, "Good gracious! Do you see papa?" One of the housemaids happened to be passing downstairs at the moment, and she was called in, and asked if she saw anything, and her reply was, "Oh, Miss! The master!" Graham—Captain Towns' old body servant—was then sent for, and he also immediately exclaimed: "Oh Lord save us! Mrs. Lett, it's the Captain!" The butler was called, and then Mrs. Crane, my wife's nurse, and they both said what they saw. Finally, Mrs. Towns was sent for and, seeing the apparition, she advanced towards it with her arm extended as if to touch it, and as she passed her hand over the panel of the wardrobe the figure gradually faded away, and never again appeared, though the room was regularly occupied for a long time after.

TRANSFORMED BY THE VISION

This statement was signed by "C.E.W. Lett," the captain's son-in-law, and came with signed affidavits of other witnesses.

In this case Bennett did not go on to measure the effects of this visionary experience on the people who saw the apparition, but it is my guess that the effect was quite profound. Many of the people I have worked with say that these visions result in an alleviation or even resolution of their grief. In the people I have helped to have apparitions, the event is primarily one of healing, in which the relationship with the deceased is improved. It is not a frightening or disturbing experience. I find this fascinating in light of the fact that films and books have taught almost all of us to fear ghosts. Ghost stories since the early days of man have been about frightening spirits who return from the dead to "get" the living, but the reality about ghost sightings is quite different. Researchers who study them have found that the experiences are not horrifying. Puzzling, yes, but the person who sees the ghost isn't driven mad with fear. Typical of sightings is the following one, a spontaneous mirror vision, which took place when a widow happened to be gazing into the mirrorlike reflection of a hotel picture window. It was dark outside, and the glass reflected the dim light from inside the room, creating a clear depth in its shiny surface:

> This happened to me shortly after my husband was killed in an automobile accident. It was early morning and I was lying in bed, staring at the window. It was still dark, so I couldn't see out; the window was just a sort of black square. I don't remember having anything in particular on my mind, I was just looking at the window.
>
> All of a sudden I could see a man running toward me. He had on a swimsuit, and his hair was wet like

7

he was running up from the beach. I became excited, because I recognized him as my dead husband! He ran right up to me and smiled. I could smell him and I know I could have felt his wet hair if I had reached out.

"Everything is fine here," he said. He was smiling and happy, and it made me happy. The experience helped me get over my grief because I was worried about the pain he must have felt when the car crashed.

In this case the wife was allowed to "close the circle" by seeing that her husband wasn't suffering in the afterlife. Her apparition, like so many, had a positive effect on her because it allowed her to process grief. It only stands to reason that a planned apparition would have greater positive effects.

THE NATURAL LINK

There are many forms of visions and many ways of facilitating them, yet visions remain among the most extraordinary phenomena of the human mind. Perhaps an odder phenomenon still is that they are seldom studied by psychologists.

Many of us have grown up in an atmosphere charged with tales of biblical visions. Who among us familiar with the Bible has not marveled at Ezekiel's wheel within a wheel; or at Jacob's ladder, or the entire book of Revelation? No wonder many of us consider these ancient visionaries to be uncommon individuals with rare and mysterious powers to commune with the divine.

These days many tend to pathologize visions. They assume that people who say they have visions are schizophrenic, or delirious, or even sociopathic. This perception is changing now, since a growing number of demographic studies show that the visionary experience is a common one in the *normal* population. Legions of people have been having visions all along. They were simply reluctant to mention them for fear of being labeled insane.

Since apparitions of the departed are a form of visionary experience, we need to consider some of the common forms of visions, especially those that can be facilitated by known methods. This narrows the field down to four: pareidolia, dream incubation, hypnagogia, and mirror visions.

The Clouded Visions of Pareidolia

The common experience of seeing faces in clouds is an example of the visual illusion known as pareidolia. It is classified as an illusion because there is an observable external stimulus—the cloud—to which an interpretation is added that leads to a meaningful image in the sky.

If I looked up in the clouds and pointed out an image of George Washington, the person standing with me would most likely see the same image. A specific distinguishing feature of pareidolia is that these illusions do not go away when we gaze at them.

Since the illusions of pareidolia are caused by an external stimulus, they can be pointed out to others. Agreement can thereby be secured among a group of people as to what the images represent. This explains some group illusions in which a large number of people suddenly see the face of Christ on the wall of a church, or the Virgin Mary on the side of an oil storage tank in the Midwest. When one person can make out the face of Christ—or any other face—in some kind of pattern, then others can see it too.

Once the image is seen, it is virtually impossible to persuade people that the pattern had really been there all along. From the point of view of those who are familiar with the site, it is as though the apparition had suddenly materialized out of nowhere. "I've been driving past that water tank almost every day for twenty years," a visionary might say. "If the Virgin Mary had been up there before, I would have seen her long before today. I know she just now appeared!"

Once word about the manifestation spreads, pilgrims often flock to the spot. Visitors to the site are usually reverent in demeanor regardless of whether they believe in the visitation or not. Perhaps the skeptics are hedging their bets.

Such imagery is not limited to the religious variety. Soda deposits and fossilized vegetation cover some areas of the Egyptian desert, giving the appearance of a forest of stone. Travelers report seeing the remains of mummified giants or great sailing ships in these formations.

Pareidolia underlies several forms of divination. The

kahunas of Hawaii occasionally posed questions to themselves and then gazed into the clouds, expecting that patterns seen there would reveal the answers they sought. Capnomancy, or divination by smoke gazing, is still practiced among the indigenous populations of Central America. In medieval Europe the practice was customarily carried out by matrons and virgins. Tea-leaf reading, too, depends upon the seers making meaningful pictures out of the tea-leaf fragments.

From time to time pareidolia has been the basis for apparitions of departed loved ones. Take the experience of General George Patton, for instance, who had an astounding vision of his ancestors while on a battlefield in France. He recounted the following episode in *Before the Colors Fade,* a memoir written by his nephew, Fred Ayer, Jr.:

"I am sure your ancestors are always with you. They are watching you. They expect a hell of a lot out of you."

I asked, "How do you mean?"

"Well, it's something you know, or you don't. But sometimes you can even see. Once in France we were pinned down by German fire, especially some heavy machine guns. I was lying flat on my belly and scared to death, hardly daring to lift my head. But finally I did, and looked up to a bank of clouds glowing reddish in the almost setting sun. And then, just as clear as clear can be, I saw their heads, the heads of my grandfather and his brothers. Their mouths weren't moving; they weren't saying anything to me. But they were looking, looking not so much in anger as with unhappy scowls. I could read their eyes and they said to me, 'Georgie, Georgie, you're a disappointment to us lying low down there. Just remember lots of Pattons have been killed, but there never was one who was a coward.'

"So I got up, drew my gun, and gave commands. And at the last Colonel George and the others were still there, but smiling. Of course, we won that particular battle."

As long as we are on the subject of General George Patton, certainly one of the most respected and successful generals in American military history, it is interesting to point out that he was a firm believer in the existence of ghosts. This belief was due in part to frequent battlefield visits he had with his departed father. As he told Ayer, "Father used to come to me in the evenings to my tent and sit down to talk and assure me that I would do all right and act bravely in the battle coming the next day. He was just as real as in his study at home at Lake Vineyard."

HEALING THROUGH DREAM INCUBATION

All of us are familiar with the caduceus, the mysterious emblem of the medical profession. Intertwined around a winged staff twin serpents stare at us from ambulance doors, hospital walls, and doctor's-office placards. Yet few of us know the meaning of this symbol. To learn that, one must go back to ancient Greece, to the dream-incubation temples of Asklepios.

Asklepios was an actual person, a revered physician who was in effect elevated to the status of a divinity after his death. Sanctuaries were erected in his honor all over his homeland. There were three hundred in all, with the most renowned being at Epidaurus, which functioned as a sort of center for dream-incubation temples.

At these temples fantastic visionary experiences were evoked for the purpose of healing. If one was afflicted with an illness that no other healer could cure, or an unbearable illness, one made the journey to a temple of Asklepios. There the sick went to have dreams and visions they hoped would cure their affliction, if they were lucky, patients would even be able to consult the legendary physician himself.

The main healing center at Epidaurus had adequate facilities to accommodate and feed the swarms of people who were always waiting their turn. The central part of the complex was a huge building called the *abaton*, which was surrounded by a courtyard. Once the time came, the pilgrims entered the courtyard and slept until they had a very specific kind of dream, one in which Asklepios, dressed in a fur coat and carrying the caduceus, appeared and invited them into the *abaton*.

The seeker could then enter the temple, a vast hall filled with narrow beds called *klinis*. These beds looked like Victorian couches, with one end elevated to about 45 degrees so that the head and trunk of the person would be elevated slightly above his or her hips and legs. It was from these *klinis* that our modern word *clinic* was derived.

Asklepios himself, it was believed, came into the *abaton* during the night. He proffered tender concern and healing, and probably did so wearing a fur coat and carrying the caduceus. In many recorded instances his prescriptions and medical procedures resulted in dramatic cures.

Grateful patients paid stonecutters to inscribe the details of their illnesses, their visions, and their cures on upright pillars so that others might learn of these miracles. Even today, more than two thousand years later, the clinical case studies that have survived make fascinating reading:

A man whose fingers, with the exception of one, were paralyzed, came as a supplicant to the god. While looking at the tablets in the Temple he expressed incredulity regarding the cures and scoffed at the inscriptions. But in his sleep he saw a vision. It seemed to him that, as he was playing at dice below the Temple and was about to cast the dice, the god appeared, sprang upon his hand, and stretched out his [the patient's] fingers. When the god had stepped aside it seemed to him [the patient] that he bent his hand and stretched out all his fingers one by one. When he had straighted them all, the god asked him if he would still be incredulous of the inscriptions on the tablets in the Temple. He answered that he would not. "Since then, formerly you were incredulous of the cures, and they were not incredible, for the future," he said, "your name shall be 'Incredulous.'" "When day dawned, he walked out sound.

Ambrosia of Athens, blind of one eye. She came as a supplicant to the god. As she walked about in the Temple she laughed at some of the cures as incredible and impossible, that the lame and the blind should be healed by merely seeing a dream. In her sleep she had a vision. It seemed to her that the god stood by her and said that he would cure her; but that in payment he would ask her to dedicate to the Temple a silver pig as a memorial of her ignorance. After saying this, he cut the diseased eyeball and poured in some drug. When day came she walked out sound:

A certain man dreamed that, struck in the belly by Asklepios with a sword, he died; this man, by means of an incision, healed the abscess which had developed in his belly.

Pandarus, a Thessalina, who had a mark on his forehead. He saw a vision as he slept. It seemed to him that the god bound the marks round with a head-band and enjoined him to remove the band when he left the *abaton* and dedicate it as an offering to the Temple. When day came he got up and took off the band and saw his face free of the marks; and he dedicated to the Temple the band with the signs which had been on his forehead.

Dream incubation was by no means confined to the Greeks. It has been recorded in many cultures around the world, such as ancient Egypt, Mesopotamia, Canaan, and Israel. The clearest biblical example is Solomon's dream at the hill shrine of Gibeon, where he went to make a burned offering to the Lord. It was there that "the Lord appeared to Solomon in a dream by night," asking what he could give to the son of David.

"Give therefore thy servant an understanding heart to judge thy people, that I may discern between good and bad; for who is able to judge this thy so great a people?"

It was this dream encounter with God that produced the wisdom of Solomon that ruled all of Israel.

The rite of dream incubation was very important in Japan, where it survived well into the fifteenth century. Pilgrims agonizing over insoluble problems journeyed to a holy site in hopes of being granted a dream by a divinity. These dreams would offer solutions to the incubant's problems.

Many accounts of these visitations have survived, and they turn out to be identical in form to those from Greece. Entities appear in the seekers' visions and perform healings that, as at the *abatons*, may involve a kind of dream surgery.

This rite goes back to a very early era in Japan, as early as the fourth and fifth centuries C.E. In those times the emperor alone was allowed this link with other dimensions, and incubation was an important aspect of his spiritual obligations. His palace was equipped with an incubation hall and a special bed known as a *kamudoko*.

Even into recent times a bed called the *shinza*, identical in configuration to the Asklepian *klini*, was required to be present during the ceremony at which the new emperor was consecrated. The emperor did not use the bed during the ritual, so its original meaning has been forgotten. No doubt in ancient times the bed was there for the purpose of incubation.

Proponents of modern depth psychology would argue that these visitations were episodes of inner communion with the incubants' higher selves, but it is impossible fully to understand the many enigmas about dream incubation.

The seekers themselves sharply differentiate these visitations from ordinary dreams. In fact many of the incubants in the accounts from ancient Greece insisted that their visions took place in a state between sleeping and waking. This brings us to another fascinating type of visionary state into which some individuals can intentionally enter.

HYPNAGOGIA'S SLEEPY REALITY

Hypnagogia is traditionally thought of as the "twilight state," a state that exists between normal waking consciousness and sleep. In hypnagogia the person sees what is being dished up by his unconscious. Sometimes it may just be bright flashes of color, or vivid dream sequences. Other times these clearer-than-life images have very powerful significance.

In this condition the hypnagogic state is reached when a person is literally walking around and performing usual tasks. Walking hypnagogia has been used to explain the reported sighting of "little people" in Ireland and "fairies" in other parts of the world. It also explains a bizarre phenomenon known as "the Disappearing Man," in which a person may see someone walking toward him on the street at night who then suddenly disappears.

Charles Dickens, the famed English author, reported one such vivid account. He told a friend that one night he was walking down a street in London when he heard a horse behind him. He turned to see a man trying to control a horse that was becoming unruly. Dickens dodged into a doorway to let the horse have the road. When he looked back, the horse and rider were gone. There was no one there.

A high percentage of the normal population has experiences of vivid imagery at the point of sleep. Sometimes these take the form of colorful images, sometimes surrealistically distorted events.

Hypnagogic states have been used by some creative geniuses to solve problems. One who used this technique in his creative process was Thomas Edison, who would frequently catnap in his office when searching for solutions.

One problem that he faced is that it is very easy to drift into full sleep from the hypnagogic state. Once asleep, one tends to forget the images experienced. To over-come this problem, Edison dozed with a steel ball in each hand. On either side of his chair he placed metal dishpans. When he started to slip into unconsciousness, the balls would fall from his hands and clang against the pans. He would then awaken with memory of his hypnagogic experience still intact.

MY OWN ENCOUNTER WITH MIRROR GAZING

After conducting a number of mirror-gazing sessions in which apparitions were facilitated, I decided to try to have one myself. The result was a personal encounter that has totally changed my perspective on life.

In the beginning this presented somewhat of a dilemma for me. I was ambivalent as to whether I should serve as an experimental subject for this project. To serve as an experimental subject and have an apparitional encounter would perhaps cause me to lose a measure of objectivity. If I limited my role to that of an investigator, I reasoned, I could evaluate the reports of the subjects from a more neutral stance.

On the other hand the temptation to try the procedure myself was very great, because from childhood I have been fascinated by consciousness and have always wanted to know what it was like to see an apparition.

After hearing a few of my subjects' accounts I succumbed to temptation and set out to take a trip of my own into the Middle Realm.

The most unsettling feature of these apparitional encounters observed from the subjects was that they were sure that their visionary reunions were real and not fantasies. This was especially perplexing in that I had intentionally selected very grounded and reasonable people as my subjects. I assumed that any of them would be able to tell whether the encounter was real. I expected them to say that the vision matched the kind of images they have while dreaming, but the opposite proved to be true. One after the other the subjects who had visionary encounters were insisting that they had actually been in the presence of their deceased relative. "I know that was my mother," said one of the subjects. Virtually all of the others described the experience as being "realer than real."

I was convinced that if I saw an apparition, it would be different. If I have an experience like that, I thought, I won't be fooled into thinking it is real.

I chose my maternal grandmother as the person I would attempt to see. I was born during World War II, and my father was shipped overseas on the day I was born. He didn't return for eighteen months, which left my mother's mother to assume many of the duties of parenting. She did a wonderful job, and I always considered her to be a sweet, wise, and understanding person who loomed large in my life. I had often missed her in the years since her death and would gladly visit with her again, in whatever form she took.

I spent many hours one day preparing for a visionary reunion with her. I brought dozens of memories to mind and looked at photographs of her, evoking a deep sense of her tender kindness.

Then I went into a place I called the apparition booth, and in the room's dim light I gazed into the depth of a large mirror, offset in such a way that I gazed into a sort of three-dimensional clarity. I did this for at least an hour, but felt not even a twinge of her presence. I finally gave up and assumed that I was somehow immune to visionary reunions.

Later, as I unwound from the experience, I had an encounter that ranks as one of the most life-changing events I have ever experienced. What happened altered my concept of reality almost totally. I now understood the sentiments expressed by many apparition watchers that they don't feel like the same person after it happens.

These experiences have an ineffable quality to them, which means they are difficult or even impossible to put into words. Still, I want to describe my own visionary reunion since I find it important to convey this experience from a first-person point of view:

I was sitting in a room alone when a woman simply walked in. As soon as I saw her, I had a certain sense that she was familiar, but the event happened so quickly that it took me a few moments to gather myself together and greet her politely. Within what must have been less than a minute, I realized this person was my *paternal* grandmother, who had died some years before. I remember throwing my hands up toward my face and exclaiming, "Grandma!"

At this point I was looking directly into her eyes, awestruck at what I was seeing. In a very kind and loving way she acknowledged who she was and addressed me with the nickname that only she had used for me when I was a child. As soon as I realized who this woman was, a flood of memories rushed into my mind. Not all of these were good memories. In fact many were distinctly unpleasant. Although my reminiscences of my maternal grandmother are positive those of my father's mother were a different matter.

One of the memories that rushed to mind was the annoying habit she had of declaring, "This is my last Christmas!" She did that every holiday season for the last two decades of her life.

She also constantly warned me when I was young that I would go to hell if I violated any of God's many strictures—as she interpreted them of course. She once washed my mouth out with soap for having uttered a word of which she disapproved. Another time when I was a child, she told me in all seriousness that it was a sin to fly in airplanes. She was habitually cranky and negative.

Yet as I gazed into the eyes of this apparition, I quickly sensed that the woman who stood before me had been transformed in a very positive way. I felt warmth and love from her as she stood there and an empathy and compassion that surpassed my understanding. She was confidently humorous, with an air of quiet calm and joyfulness about her.

The reason I had not recognized her at first was that she appeared much younger than she was when she died, in fact even younger than she had been when I was born. I don't remember having seen any photographs of her at the age she seemed to be during this encounter, but that is irrelevant here since it was not totally through her physical appearance that I recognized her. Rather, I knew this woman through her unmistakable presence and through the many memories we reviewed and discussed. In short this woman was my deceased grandmother. I would have known her anywhere.

I want to emphasize how completely natural this meeting was. As with the other subjects who had experienced an apparitional facilitation, my meeting was in no way eerie or bizarre. In fact this was the most normal and satisfying interaction I have ever had with her.

Our meeting was focused entirely on our relationship. Throughout the experience I was amazed that I seemed to be in the presence of someone who had already passed on, but in no way did this interfere with our interaction. She was there in front of me, and as startling as that fact was, I just accepted it and continued to talk with her.

We discussed old times, specific incidents from my childhood. Throughout she reminded me of several events that I had forgotten. Also she revealed something very personal about my family situation that came as a great surprise but in retrospect makes a great deal of sense. Due to the fact that the principals are still living, I have chosen to keep this information to myself. But I will say that her revelation has made a great deal of difference in my life, and I feel much better for having heard this from her.

I say "heard" in an almost literal sense. I did hear her voice clearly, the only difference being that there was a crisp, electric quality to it that seemed clearer and louder than her voice before she died. Others who'd had this experience before me described it as telepathic or "mind to mind" communication. Mine was similar. Although most of my conversation was through the spoken word, from time to time I was immediately aware of what she was thinking, and I could tell that the same was true for her.

In no way did she appear "ghostly" or transparent during our reunion. She seemed completely solid in every respect. She appeared no different from any other person except that she was surrounded by what appeared to be a light or an indentation in space, as if she were somehow set off or recessed from the rest of her physical surroundings.

For some reason, though, she would not let me touch her. Two or three times I reached to give her a hug, and each time she put her hands up and motioned me back. She was so insistent about not being touched that I didn't pursue it.

I have no idea how long this meeting lasted in clock time. It certainly seemed like a long time, but I was so engrossed in the experience that I didn't bother to look at the clock. In terms of thoughts and feelings that passed between us, it seemed like a couple of hours, but I have a feeling that it was probably less than that in what we consider to be "real" time.

And how did our meeting end? I was so overwhelmed that I just said, "Good-bye." We acknowledged that we would be seeing each other again, and I simply walked out of the room. When I returned, she was nowhere to be seen. The apparition of my grandmother was gone.

What took place that day resulted in a healing of our relationship. For the first time in my life I now appreciate her humor and have a sense of some of the struggles she went through during her lifetime. Now I love her in a way that I didn't before the experience.

It also left me with an abiding certainty that what we call death is not the end of life.

I realize how people can assume that these apparitional facilitations are hallucinations. As a veteran of altered states of consciousness, I can say that my visionary reunion with my grandmother was completely coherent with the ordinary waking reality that I have experienced all my life. If I were to discount this encounter as hallucinatory, I would be almost obliged to discount the rest of my life as hallucinatory too.

THE "NEED TO SEE" BASIS

My encounter has clarified why it is that apparition seekers do not necessarily see the person whom they have set out to see. On the basis of my own experience, I believe that the subjects see the person they *need* to see.

In my case the relationship was smooth between my maternal grandmother and me, whereas things were rocky in my relationship with my paternal grandmother. Generally, greater benefits probably result from reunions with people with whom one still has difficulties.

For many subjects the person whom they desire to see is the same as the one they need to see. If the two coincide, the reunion goes as planned; if they do not, need may prevail.

Also, one detail of my experience makes it necessary to offer a public apology to my old friend Dr. Elisabeth Kübler-Ross. In 1977 Elisabeth told me a story about her own encounter with a deceased acquaintance. As I recall the story, Elisabeth was walking in a hallway toward her office one day when she happened to notice a woman standing in the corridor.

The two women struck up a conversation, and Elisabeth led the woman into her office. After a while Elisabeth leaned toward the woman and, with considerable amazement, said, "I know you!" She had recognized the woman to be a "Mrs. Schwartz," a patient to whom she had been close and who had died some months earlier. Mrs. Schwartz acknowledged her identity, and the two continued to talk for some period of time.

When Elisabeth told me this story, I remember protesting loudly. "Elisabeth, give me a break!" I said. "If this was someone you knew so well, how could it be that you didn't recognize her from the beginning?"

Now, all these years later, I can say that I understand. From my own experience and those of others I can confirm that apparitions of the deceased don't look exactly as they did before they died. Strangely—or perhaps not so—they look younger and less stressed in their apparitional state, but still they are recognizable as who they are.

The results of my own experience and early experimentation suggest to me that mirror gazing is a natural link between spontaneous and facilitated apparitions of the departed.

Further research has convinced me that mirror gazing was used in historic times with amazing results. It was this historic evidence that got me even more involved in mirror gazing.

THE SUPPRESSION OF MIRROR GAZING

Through my research and involvement I have come to realize that mirror gazing has been subjected through the centuries to such a barrage of bannings and defamations that it now survives as only a remnant of the living social reality it once was. It is an echo of the distant past, dismissed by those who have called it superstition rather than try to understand its appeal and power.

A story that illustrates the thankless nature of mirror gazing is the tragic tale of Kenneth MacKenzie. He was a mirror gazer in fifteenth-century Scotland who was known to be such an expert that a local queen (there were many in this feudal society) hired him to spy on her husband, who was visiting the European continent. MacKenzie gazed into his speculum and saw the king happily cavorting with another woman.

What he saw proved to be true, but Mackenzie's mistake was in telling the queen. She became so angry at the vision that she had MacKenzie executed by throwing him headfirst into a barrel of boiling tar.

So it has been for the practitioners of mirror gazing.

In the course of my research I have been able to

uncover at least seven reasons why society has tried to suppress mirror gazing. In what follows I will state these reasons and then examine them with an eye toward determining whether or not they are sound, individually and/or collectively.

FEAR OF THE UNCONSCIOUS

There seem to be dimensions of the mind of which we are not ordinarily aware. Freud and Jung and other pioneers of psychology have mapped out a number of these regions, and the process will no doubt go on. There is, after all, still much to learn about the human mind.

One of the things that is known is that anxiety often arises when some unpleasant thought, memory, or impulse threatens to emerge from the unconscious mind into conscious awareness. Freud called this common experience *signal anxiety*.

One reason mirror gazing is considered taboo by some is the fear that the mind's unconscious contents will erupt into consciousness. What people fear is that if these unconscious memories or feelings come to light, something dreadful will happen. Some fear they will become emotionally overwhelmed, or lose control of themselves, or perhaps embarrass themselves in some irretrievable way.

Unconscious thoughts do surface during mirror gazing, but this emergence is by no means the awful event some imagine. Usually it is beneficial, contributing to growth and development.

Though some people denounce mirror gazing because it calls up threatening thoughts or impulses, my experience is that it should be praised for this. My point is well illustrated by a story reported by the classical scholar W. R. Halliday in his 1913 book *Greek Divination*. This is the only account that I have been able to uncover in seven years of diligent research on mirror gazing in which an untoward psychological event occurred in a person in association with mirror gazing.

In this account Halliday calls gazing a "superstition" and then goes on to state that it has been "exploited with more serious and tragic results among the uneducated classes who have not had equal opportunities of acquiring discernment. The *Manchester Guardian* of October 28, 1909, contained an account of a coroner's inquest on a Cardiff postman's wife who committed suicide by inhaling gas. Her stepfather gave evidence that the week before she had come back from a visit to a fortune teller and had said, 'When he asked me to look in the crystal, I saw myself seated in a chair deliberately committing suicide with gas.'"

The moral Halliday draws from this sad tale is clearly that one should not abide mirror gazers. I am sure that most mental-health professionals would realize that this woman's mirror vision did not cause her suicide, as Halliday seems to imply. In fact the causal relationship is the other way around: her vision and in all probability her visit to the fortune-teller were both the result of her depression. She was depressed to the point of suicide *before* going to the fortune-teller. What she saw in the mirror was merely a mirror of the thoughts in her unconscious mind.

One may conclude from Halliday's account that mirror gazing has potential as a method of detecting and diagnosing mental and emotional disorders, in this case depression.

THEOLOGICAL REASONS

Throughout the ages religious officials have banned the practice of mirror gazing because they feel it involves the operation of demonic forces.

A long series of church councils and institutions have reinforced this belief. For example, as early as the fifth century a synod held by Saint Patrick declared that any Christian who believes that a spirit can be seen in a mirror shall be anathematized and must be excluded from the church until he or she renounces this belief and performs penance.

Hinmarus, a ninth-century archbishop in France, condemned hydromancy—gazing in water in order to have visions. In 1398 itinerant mirror gazers, called specularii, were declared by the Paris Faculty of Theology to be minions of Satan.

Count Cagliostro was imprisoned by the Inquisition officials in Rome for his practices, foremost among which was mirror gazing. Such condemnation has continued even into the contemporary world. According to a 1979 press account, two women were banished from a Baptist church in Independence, Missouri, because they told fortunes by means of a crystal ball.

Religious establishments depend heavily for their continuance on instilling rigid ideological beliefs about body, mind, and spirit in their members. This includes discouraging them from seeking spiritual experiences on their own. After all, a psychological pioneer in the congregation who explores hidden realms of the self may well make discoveries that are difficult to reconcile with official doctrines.

As for the intimations of some in the religious community that the forces of evil are itching to corrupt us through the mirror, I suspect they are attempts to scare us into ideological conformity or are disguised manifestations of the same fear of the unconscious mind we discussed earlier.

I am sure that mine are not the last words on the subject of devils. And I mean it seriously when I say that I intend no disrespect to serious thinkers who argue for the existence of objective evil. In terms of the specific issue of mirror gazing, I can only say that a serious theological anomaly arises when church authorities link it with demonic practice, for at least one of the Bible's holiest figures most likely used forms of mirror gazing to get in touch with the divine. Joseph mirror-gazed in a, silver cup that he carried with him.

Still, there are at least five biblical passages in which evocation of the deceased is condemned, in three instances in words attributed to God himself. Here they are:

31

Do not resort to ghosts and spirits, nor make yourselves unclean by seeking them out. I am the Lord your God.

—Lev. 19:31

[The Lord says] I will set my face against the man who wantonly resorts to ghosts and spirits, and I will cut that person off from his people.

—Lev. 20:6

Any man or woman among you who calls up ghosts or spirits shall be put to death. The people shall stone them; their blood shall be on their own heads.

—Lev. 20:27

There is no mistaking the meaning of these passages. Upon reading the verses in the context of the two chapters in which they appear, I feel less that I have violated the word of God and more that I have found another of those areas in which ancient values have collided with modern times. Here are the passages in their broader context:

The Lord spoke to Moses and said . . . You shall not allow two different kinds of beasts to mate together. You shall not plant your field with two kinds of seed. You shall not put on garments woven with two kinds of yarn . . . You shall not round off your hair from side to side, and you shall not shave the edge of your beards . . . You shall not tattoo yourselves. I am the

Lord . . . Do not resort to ghosts and spirits, nor make yourselves unclean by seeking them out. I am the Lord your God . . . You shall not pervert justice in measurement of length, weight or quantity. You shall have true scales, true weights, true measures dry and liquid . . . I will set my face against the man who wantonly resorts to ghosts and spirits, and I will cut that person off from his people . . . If a man commits adultery with his neighbor's wife, both adulterer and adulteress shall be put to death.

And so on. When fundamentalists bring up the biblical objections to "ghosts and spirits," I am quick to reach for the Bible and read to them in their proper context the passages they cite. To follow the teachings expressed in just the portion I have quoted would mean that a true follower could not wear clothing made of blended material, cut his hair, shave his beard, wear tattoos, plant more than one crop in a plot of ground, and so forth.

MIRROR GAZERS AS CHARLATANS

Mirror gazing has been associated with chicanery and fraud, and the historical record leaves no doubt that in part this is justified. It is clear that certain self-proclaimed mirror gazers have engaged in conscious deception of others for personal gain.

Popular literature has reflected this theme as well. Who can forget the bogus fortune-teller in *The Wizard of Oz*, the one who made steam, noise, and anger come from his control booth behind the curtain? "I am the wizard!" shouted this mere mortal, making his image appear much larger and more frightening on a huge movie screen.

This is not unlike the Catholic bishop Hippolytus. In the words of classical scholar E. R. Dodds, "Hippolytus includes in his collection of conjuring tricks a device which could be used to fake both visual and auditory automatism: a cauldron of water with a glass bottom is placed over a small skylight, and the [gazer], gazing into the cauldron, sees [and perhaps hears?] in its depths certain demons, who are really the magician's accomplices seated in the room below."

Because of such abuses society has seen fit to establish laws to protect people against unscrupulous mirror gazers, but none of this can serve to justify the indiscriminate banning of mirror gazing.

Indeed, the fact that the public is misinformed about the nature of mirror visions makes it even easier for charlatans to deceive their victims. Plainly charlatans are able to lay claim to unusual powers in such circumstances by the simple expedient of "producing" these phenomena.

By the way, I have had some people come to me who thought that mirror gazing was a fraud. Still, they had the courage to try experimentation and found their efforts rewarded with success.

For example, after I had delivered a lecture in Seattle on this subject, a skeptical medical doctor declared that mirror visions were simply the product of suggestion. He implied that "right-thinking" people couldn't experience these visions. I had him accompany me back to my hotel room, where I closed the curtains and dimmed the lights. I had him sit at an angle to a mirror in the room to provide a clear depth. I had him relax as he gazed into the mirror. Despite his doubt, he proved to be an excellent subject. Within a few minutes he reported clouds in the speculum followed by geometric shapes. When faces appeared, he terminated the session. "I see what you mean," he said, subdued by the experience. "It does work."

CONFLICTS WITH MODERN TECHNOLOGY

In the modern world our daily lives are so closely integrated with technological creations that most of us would probably not survive without our machines.

This reliance upon technology has brought about a faster pace of life, one that would have been unimaginable a hundred years ago. This faster pace has the effect of discouraging people from enjoying the delights of altered states of awareness, many of which require you to slow down and think differently from the way you have become accustomed to.

Technological developments have obviated some of the earlier uses of mirror gazing. Such devices as the television and telephone and professions such as psychiatry have taken the place of the will and the need to delve into one's unconscious mind for insight as well as for entertainment.

Mirror gazing requires a different mind-set from the one currently plotted for us in our daily lives. That is why preparation for it includes slowing down the pace of living and actually trying to enter, if you will, an other time frame.

I have created an environment to take people out of the modern era and back to a time that was slower and more compatible with the altered state we are trying to induce. You will have to do the same thing in your own environment to properly facilitate an apparition.

MIRROR GAZING AS UNSCIENTIFIC

The scientific method is a specialized mode of observing, thinking, and reasoning that depends heavily on a kind of alert, focused, critical, and reflective state of mind.

Since much of our environment in the contemporary world has its origin in the scientific method, it is not surprising that scientific thinking has come to be officially sanctioned. There are many people who regard all other ways of thought as somehow faulted or dubious.

There is much to be said for this attitude, since a glance backward at history is enough to make us profoundly grateful for the emergence of scientific thought.

However, the contemporary scientific worldview, grounded as it is in critical thought, is somewhat contemptuous of altered states of consciousness. Most scientists believe that critical-reflective awareness is allied with truth, whereas other levels of consciousness are "unreal" or "deceptive," even "illusory" or "hallucinatory." Since mirror gazing is based upon hypnagogic awareness, scientists tend to dismiss it out of hand.

A closer analysis of the progress of science reveals that there are numerous instances in which scientists have gathered inspiration from the hypnagogic state. Among these are Thomas Edison, Kekule, and René Descartes. The last created what is known as the scientific method, by which all good scientific experimentation is conducted, as the result of a series of vivid dreams! Descartes' dreams are a marvelous example of interpretative intellect being combined with the offerings of the unconscious mind.

In the first dream wind is whirling around Descartes as he struggles down the street trying to reach a church to say his prayers. He notices that he has passed an acquaintance without having greeted him and tries to return, but the wind won't let him. He then sees another man standing outside the church who tells him that another of his friends is waiting in the church to give him a melon. Descartes awakens and concludes that the dream is the work of an evil demon. He prays to God for protection and goes back to sleep.

In the next dream he hears a loud sound that he takes to be a clap of thunder. Immediately awake, he sees thousands of fiery sparks in the room.

In the third dream he finds a dictionary on his table and next to it a collection of poems entitled *Corpus Poetarum*. Opening the book of poems, he reads the line "What path shall I follow in life?" A man he does not know presents him with verses that begin with the words "yes and no."

When Descartes awoke, he concluded that the three dreams were divinely inspired. The first two were warnings about the way he had lived up until that day, November 10, 1619. The third was a symbol of encouragement for his mission in life, to set the sciences on a path to knowledge.

It is now clear what Descartes meant when he wrote, "I one day resolved to take myself too as an object of study." To Descartes the scientific method became known as "the natural light of reason."

MIRROR GAZING AND "OFFICIAL" REALITY

Although we acknowledge that everyone's reality is different, it is nonetheless true that there is an "officially sanctioned" concept of reality.

The great philosophers and scientists whose thoughts have shaped our modern view of the world have drawn a distinct line between "reality" and "unreality." That line works most of the time, but problems arise when something crosses that line. Dreams, for instance, are held by many thinkers as classic examples of something unreal. Similarly, in the process of development, children are taught that dreams are unreal.

I suggest that some people are puzzled by mirror gazing and similar phenomena because these call into question our culturally ingrained version of what is real and unreal. Indeed sometimes the people who have them are puzzled by what is happening. But when they think about it, they find value in the images they have seen. As with dreams mirror visions have deep meaning.

Everyone has a unique reality. To my way of thinking, mirror visions are not "unreal." Rather they are a means of exploring true reality more effectively.

A SEEDY GAME

Today mirror gazing is seen as a parlor game or a fixture of amusement parks and seedy boardwalks. These unsavory impressions are not sufficient reasons to reject mirror gazing. At its best it is a valuable therapeutic tool for overcoming grief and attaining levels of self-discovery. Even if it is simply regarded as a pastime, mirror gazing is a legitimate form of recreation and a fascinating exercise.

I believe that by mastering the art of mirror gazing, one can democratize the visionary process. No longer will long hours of therapy be required to explore psychological problems that stem from the unconscious mind. Rather one's deepest emotions can be reached by a therapist skilled in the art of mirror gazing.

EXPLORERS BEWARE

If you plan to delve into this area, I warn you to be prepared to encounter angry reactions from those around you. This response came as a complete surprise to me. Although people often commend me for the courage they believe it must have taken to study and write about near-death experiences, I was never scorned by skeptical scientists and physicians, and I did not suffer that much persecution for my earlier research.

It has been different in the case of my present work. When I told one psychologist about my plans to conduct this study, he said, "There goes your career!" An intelligent woman friend characterized the project as "stupid and funny" and even forbade me to speak of the subject in her presence.

The most ominous response came in December 1991 when I was checked into a hospital for an extremely high thyroid level, a condition known as hyperthyroidism.

Why this happened is still a mystery to me. I have taken thyroid pills since 1985, when it was found that my body was not producing enough of the vital hormone. For some reason this dosage suddenly proved to be too much, and I became delirious.

I was admitted to a hospital so that the doctors could adjust my dosage of synthroid, a synthetically produced form of thyroid.

While I was there, I made the mistake of asking a doctor if he could photocopy a summary of a presentation I had written on mirror gazing. I was going to present the results of my research to the members of an international education institute, and they needed a copy of my speech so that they could summarize it for a forthcoming speaker's bulletin.

When the physician returned from the copy machine, he tersely remarked that he had made a copy for himself. He said it was vivid proof that I had "gone off the deep end." Despite my known history of hypothyroidism, he now made the diagnosis of manic-depressive illness and prescribed lithium!

I refused the new medication, and my symptoms cleared up within a few days as my thyroxine level returned to normal. A few months later, when I gave my talk to the educators, it was very well received.

This encounter gave me the firsthand realization that fundamentalists are the ones who have always been stirred to fear and loathing when it comes to ideas such as mirror gazing. Fundamentalists of whatever stripe, be it Christian, Jew, psychiatrist, or psychologist, are people who become transfixed by a cognitive structure, meaning that they obsess on an inflexible system of beliefs. They protest against new ideas or inventions that somehow impinge on their rigid inner strictures. Religious fundamentalists will voice their old refrain: "This is the work of Satan!" Psychological fundamentalists have similar refrains as well: "I have never seen this, so it can't be true."

It is clear to me that insecurity underlies this attitude. Rather than being open-minded and willing to search for answers, fundamentalists are fervent ideologues who appear to be defending themselves against doubt and uncertainty. They refuse to acknowledge that there are some aspects of human psychology that we know very little about And they certainly don't want people to know how much fun they can have with psychology, especially something such as mirror gazing, which might allow them to settle problems for themselves in an enjoyable way.

A DOUBLE-EDGED SWORD

You might think that devoted believers in the paranormal appreciate my work in visionary facilitation. That hasn't been entirely true. A number of them have expressed qualms about my work. Perhaps they sensed that investigations that hold out the promise of confirming claims about apparitions also threaten to refute those claims.

This attitude isn't fair. We fans of the paranormal need to face up to the possibility that cherished occult doctrines may be subjected to major tests if apparitions of the deceased are ever monitored in a laboratory setting.

There is a powerful contingent of scientists who would prefer that altered states not be researched. These people, whom Aldous Huxley called "dreadful consequences argufiers," propose that if we give things such as mirror gazing the least bit of credence, we run a grave risk of resurrecting the entire gamut of magical thinking that might result in a giant step backward into the Dark Ages.

There is no reason why this should be. When it comes to such a complex, fascinating, and anxiety-provoking phenomenon as mirror gazing, only a completely forthright analysis is likely to be satisfactory. Besides, further research convinced me that mirror gazing was used in historic times with amazing results. It was this historic evidence that drew me even further into mirror gazing.

TWO

GAZING THROUGH HISTORY

Know Thyself.
—Ancient aphorism over the temple at Delphi

The people of ancient Greece were heroic and accomplished navigators of the Middle Realm, but few among them were more resourceful than the wise and beloved Salmoxis. He was a man who evoked a posthumous apparition—of himself!

Salmoxis lived before 500 B.C. in Thrace. When he was a young man, Salmoxis was enslaved for reasons we do not know. As a slave he had the good fortune to end up in the service of Pythagoras. Pythagoras was one of the great thinkers of ancient Greece. He believed that numbers are the ultimate elements of the universe. He was also a believer in life after death.

Apparently he spent much time talking to his slave about this concept. When Salmoxis became a free man, he also found himself a firm believer in an afterlife.

Salmoxis left Thrace for several years and returned a

rich man. The first thing he did upon returning was to build a theater. This theater was devoted to the discussion of topics that dealt with parapsychology. Since Salmoxis had a dramatic bent to his presentations, I have no doubt that his was somewhat of a theater of the mind.

He lectured to the people about life after death. He assured them that there is no reason to feel bad about dying. There is life after death, he told them, presenting arguments for the existence of the soul.

The people of Thrace loved Salmoxis, and he loved them. He became a great benefactor to the community. Salmoxis was recognized everywhere he went, and nowhere in the scant historical record about this man is there uttered an unkind word.

He lectured about life after death for many years. And all the while he was digging an underground chamber. Actually it was more than just a chamber; it was a subterranean house. Perhaps he constructed his habitat over a gurgling spring and stocked it with chickens and great vats of olives and a fine collection of venerable scrolls and torches with which to read them.

When the underground house was completed, Salmoxis very publicly sealed himself inside. This must have been done with great pomp and ceremony. Although there is no account of the actual event, I would guess that Salmoxis spoke at length about the afterlife and then went into this homemade replica of the Underworld, where the Greeks thought we went when we died. To the horror and sorrow of the crowd, the opening was covered with a stone slab. It was as though their great friend had died.

Salmoxis stayed underground for a long time. The historical record as written by Herodotus shows that Salmoxis may have stayed as long as three years.

Above him the people mourned. They wept and carried on. Some went day after day to his theater and prayed to the gods for his deliverance. I think that the scene must have been like a long-running soap opera.

"Is he alive? Could he possibly stay down there this long?" the people probably said. "Will we ever see him again? Do you think he's still alive down there?"

They mourned him as though he had died. And indeed the great insight of Salmoxis was that a separation *is* a death.

Finally, three years later, he reemerged. He came right out of the ground to the cheers of the citizens of Thrace and rejoined society.

Herodotus, the first known historian, wrote about this Lazarus-like event and interpreted it this way: "And thereby he proved to them the truth of what he had said. That death is no cause for worry."

When we read that statement from a rational point of view, it looks absolutely absurd. But when we examine it emotionally, it is true. Salmoxis did show that "death is no cause for worry."

After the people had witnessed the social death of Salmoxis, they would go through their mourning process as though he were actually dead. They would express denial that Salmoxis was really gone, and some would even have lingering anger at the loss of their good friend.

Some might even have made promises to the gods in order to bargain him back from the Underworld.

When he returned, their angst would be resolved. After that the people of Thrace could not be convinced that there was anything to worry about in death.

Salmoxis completed the cycle of grief for the people of Thrace. He did what can be done with mirror gazing, only in a different way. He traversed into that middle zone that exists between life and death.

FERTILE INNER VOYAGES

This ancient culture was fertile ground from which to launch such fantastic inner voyages. It is plain from the historical record that the Greeks accepted that under certain circumstances they could raise and even interact with the spirits of the dead.

To do this, they set aside psychomanteums, or oracles of the dead, where the crossover between this realm and the next could be made.

Homer, on the other hand, has given us a graphic account of a ceremony for summoning the dead that didn't require the elaborate facilities and ritual that were found at the oracles of the dead. Following a recipe given to him by the sorceress Circe, Odysseus sailed to an oracle that was consecrated for this activity. Here the brave traveler dug a shallow pit that he then filled with the blood from a sacrificial ewe and ram, a pool of blood into which he gazed and communicated with the spirits.

Then the souls of the dead who had passed away came up in a crowd from Erebos: young men and brides, old men who had suffered much, and tender maidens to whom sorrow was a new thing; others killed in battle, warriors clad in bloodstained armour. All this crowd gathered about the pit from every side, with a dreadful great noise, which made me pale with fear.

Following this encounter Odysseus has a conversation with his mother, who, unbeknownst to him, has died in a faraway land. Odysseus assumes that his mother's death has been a violent one, or perhaps one brought about by lingering illness, but she denies both of these possible causes. "It was no disease that made me pine away," says his mother. "But I missed you so much, and your clever wit and your gay merry ways, and life was sweet no longer, so I died."

"When I heard this, I longed to throw my arms round her neck," says Odysseus. "Three times I tried to embrace the ghost, three times it slipt through my hands like a shadow or a dream."

I surmise that the blood provided a reflective surface in which Odysseus was seeing mirror visions of the deceased. In his day Homer's readers would have known about such practices and would have understood immediately what Odysseus was doing. The poet Homer, who told the heroic story of Odysseus, would have no more need to describe the process of mirror gazing than would a contemporary novelist need to describe the watching of television to contemporary readers.

EXCAVATING AN ORACLE OF THE DEAD

It is significant that Homer locates this event on the river Acheron, near "the city of the Cimmerian people." Herodotus wrote of an oracle of the dead that was apparently located in the same place. This institution, also known as a psychomanteum, was located in the city of Ephyra in Epirus, an area in western Greece.

Strabo, the ancient Greek geographer, also declared that this oracle of the dead was run by the Cimmerians. He said that they dwelled in underground clay houses interconnected by tunnels. By ancestral custom those who lived in the immediate vicinity of the oracle never came out into the daylight, venturing forth from their caverns only by night. Homer must have imagined their occupation to be a gloomy one, for he pitied them by saying, "Abominable night is for ever spread over those unhappy mortals."

In late late 1950s Sotiris Dakaris, a Greek archaeologist, rediscovered and began to excavate the site. The oracle turned out to be an elaborate subterranean complex, a maze of passageways and chambers that opened at last into a lengthy and cavernous hallway in which the apparitions were seen.

In this hall Dakaris found the remnants of an enormous bronze cauldron surrounded by a railing. He speculated that this railing prevented the oracle seekers from crowding too close and concluded that the priests who ran the facility concealed themselves in the cauldron and acted out the part of the spirits of those whom the seekers were expecting to see.

I have a different interpretation.

The custom of using cauldrons, bowls, basins, cups, and other vessels filled with liquid as specula for mirror gazing is an ancient practice that is spread over many cultures. If made of metal, as this cauldron was, such containers could be highly polished, rendering them even more effective for the purpose of mirror gazing.

It is my guess that the inside of the cauldron would probably have been polished and the apparitions would have been seen in the reflective surface of the water-filled vessel. The round shape would have made it possible for several people to encircle it and to gaze simultaneously into the clear depth. The massive size of the cauldron would have created huge, life-size apparitions, since the size of the vision is directly related to the size of the speculum.

Phillipp Vandenberg wrote of the thorough and extensive preparation given people who went to inquire of the oracle. They were essentially imprisoned underground for a month and conducted through dark corridors and chambers before being allowed into the apparition chamber, where their long-term solitude in darkness would be broken by flickering firelight that cast eerie shadows on the wall. This elaborate preparation of the people going into the apparition hallway is another indication to me that the cauldron was not filled with fraudulent priests.

After gazing into the cauldron and presumably having an apparitional experience, seekers were fumigated with sulfur, traditionally used to purify anyone who had had contact with the dead. Then they were taken outside into the daylight and down to the river for a ritual bath.

THE INFLUENCE ON PLATO

If Vandenberg's account is correct, then I have an exciting speculation. Is it not possible that Plato's haunting Allegory of the Cave is actually a parody of the Oracle of the Dead at Ephyra? In the *Republic*, the ancient philosopher was writing about the limits of human knowledge and our general ignorance of Reality. He used the allegory to teach that it is as if we live in a cave and do not know what wonders lie just above us on the surface of the earth. The Oracle of Ephyra provides many similar images. People are imprisoned in a subterranean cavern, shadows are cast on the walls by flickering flames, attendants are bent on convincing their clients that the shadows are real, and when the captives are at last liberated, they are led first to the surface of the earth and then to a body of water.

Plato was an accomplished parodist, a talent he demonstrated especially in his middle dialogues. He even lampooned his fellow philosophers, some of whom remain known today only through Plato's caricatures of them.

The Oracle of the Dead at Ephyra was clearly

functioning during his lifetime, and despite the fact that it was in a very out-of-the-way location, there is abundant evidence that people flocked there in great numbers. We cannot doubt that so well informed a man as Plato would have known all about it, nor can we doubt that this popular attraction could have been grist for his mill.

Could it have been the Oracle of the Dead at Ephyra that Plato used in Book VII of the *Republic*? Consider this passage:

> Let me show in a figure how far our nature is enlightened or unenlightened:—Behold! human beings living in an underground den, which has a mouth open toward the light and reaching all along the den; here they have been from their childhood, and have their legs and necks chained so that they cannot move, and can only see before them, being prevented by the chains from turning round their heads. Above and behind them a fire is blazing at a distance, and between the fire and the prisoners there is a raised way; and you will see, if you look, a low wall built along the way, like the screen which marionette players have in front of them, over which they show puppets.

I submit that this darkly stirring allegory is on one level a parody of the Oracle of the Dead at Ephyra. The two situations are clearly parallel at several points. In both, the strange inhabitants of a subterranean world never see the light of day. Anonymous attendants deceive prisoners into believing that shadows cast by flickering flames on the walls of caverns are real. The captives are at last liberated and led first into the light of the sun and then to a body of water.

There are textual hints that Plato is satirizing the Oracle of the Dead as well. Early in the *Republic* Socrates seems to allude to the incident in which Periander sent a delegation to Ephyra to summon his wife from the Underworld. The dialogue begins with an attempt to define justice as returning to others what one has received from them. He demolishes this definition, saying it was probably proposed by Periander or someone like him. The irony is plain here: Periander was obviously an unjust man who went to the extraordinary length of having his wife summoned from the dead in order to be able to return something a friend had left in his care.

Most analyses of the allegory focus on the plight of the prisoners, but Socrates mentions others dwelling in the cave—namely, the attendants who produce the shadows in order to deceive the prisoners. I think these attendants are the guides who conducted the apparition seekers through their visionary quest, while the prisoners represent the apparition seekers themselves. It is possible that the guides were the Cimmerian people, who by custom lived forever in the dark.

I suspect that Plato did have the Oracle of the Dead at Ephyra in mind when he wrote his famous myth. Unfortunately, though, many questions remain unanswered because of the calamitous events that overtook Ephyra.

In 280 B.C.E., Pyrrhus, the King of Epirus, heroically set out with an army of twenty-five thousand men and defeated the Roman army. One year later he beat the Romans again, but he lost so many men in that battle that his army was almost destroyed. "One more victory," he remarked, "and we are defeated." Hence the origin of the phrase *Pyrrhic victory*, which means that one can lose for winning.

The brave victories of Pyrrhus were such an embarrassment to the Romans that a century later they invaded Epirus and laid waste to seventy cities. Among those cities destroyed was Ephyra. Although ruins of the oracle still exist; records of events that had taken place inside were destroyed. What remains for those of us in the twentieth century are the ruins themselves, a few sparse historical, literary, and anthropological sources—all interesting, but little more than echoes from the past

A TRAVELER'S GUIDE TO
THE MIDDLE REALM

Those who become engrossed in this subject may want to visit the Oracle of the Dead at Ephyra, Even today it is off the beaten track in a mountainous region of Greece. In the days of antiquity travels to the Oracle of the Dead must have been unbelievably arduous. It was meant to be an ordeal, since such a long trip would surely provide a heightened sense of anticipation for the apparition seeker.

My wife and I had a great deal of difficulty finding the

Oracle of the Dead when we traveled to Greece in March 1993 to spend a day at civilization's first established psychomanteum.

To get there from Athens, we first traveled northward by air to the city of Ioánnina. After an overnight stay we took a bus to Préveza, a two-hour trip that was followed immediately by a bus trip to the small town of Kanaliki.

These bus trips are not for the fainthearted. Significant portions of them wind around tight curves that leave the passengers gaping out the window at seemingly bottomless canyons.

The trip has more than fear to offer. There is beautiful countryside and colorful scenes of rural Greece.

When at last in Kanaliki, we caught a taxi to the *necromanteion*, which is what the locals call it. It is about four miles outside of town and is perched atop a prominent hill beneath a Byzantine chapel that was built in medieval times, possibly to conceal the oracle with a Christian edifice. The oracle remained covered with dirt for hundreds of years. Recently it has been excavated, and most of the ruins are now clearly visible.

The driver dropped us off a few feet from the gate of the steel fence that surrounds the ancient ruins. We asked him to return, which proved to be a lucky move, since, at the time of our visit, there was no telephone at the site.

There were also no other visitors. My wife and I were alone on the spot immortalized by Odysseus and Orpheus and visited by thousands of people in their quest to see lost loved ones. With the blessings of Socrates, the humorous gentleman who has been the caretaker of the oracle for almost twenty-five years, we were allowed to roam freely through the remains of this early spiritual retreat.

The roof of the structure is gone, leaving exposed the maze of corridors and rooms that apparition seekers wandered through while waiting to venture into the apparition chamber. All of the portions of the oracle are still visible. We sat in the living quarters of the priests— called *psychopomps*—who ran the facility. Their rooms were large by the standards of the ancients, yet measured no more than ten feet by ten feet. Leaving the priests' quarters and winding through the maze of corridors, I tried to imagine what this place would have been like two thousand years ago when it was as dark as a cave and filled with a kind of eerie anticipation. What did people do for the weeks they were in here? What did they think about and talk about? Even though I like to be alone, my mind boggled at the thought of such lengthy and total sensory deprivation.

The dormitories where the apparition seekers slept were easily found. So, too, was the apparitional chamber. It was the largest room in the maze, with high walls and a broad floor. Standing in this room, I could imagine what a rush to the senses it would be to enter this room after nearly a month of semidarkness. In this majestic chamber torches would be flickering against the walls as robed priests guided apparition seekers to the polished metal cauldron that dominated the room. At the rim of the cauldron they would be told to gaze into the shimmering metal and behold the vision that they came to see.

Standing in the middle of this room where the cauldron must have been, I could just imagine what the priests witnessed as person after person saw their apparitions. From my work at my own psychomanteum thousands of miles away, I knew that the faces of these subjects must have been filled with joy and puzzlement over the magical visions and the air filled with shrieks of delight as lost family and lovers returned for just a few moments more.

Standing above the ruins, I realized what an architectural feat this psychomanteum must have been for the ancients. They built it with great care and strength, so much so that it stands to this day as a monument to the important role that evocation of the dead played in that culture.

FROM RELIGION TO QUEEN ELIZABETH

Since existing accounts of mirror gazing remain sparse, it is almost impossible to provide a historical delineation of it without gaps. Unlike the history of such subjects as chemistry or philosophy, there is no continuous tradition extending back hundreds of years.

Instead mirror gazing seems to erupt in fits and starts, appearing here and there and then vanishing—scattered outbreaks rather than an uninterrupted line of transmission. Nonetheless when it *has* sprung up, it has often had an interesting effect.

The best I can do is provide a series of vignettes in which mirror vision has played a role in human culture. These vignettes are taken from literature, myth, religion, politics, and everyday life. Although this history at times skips hundreds of years, it will be clear that the use of mirror gazing to conjure spirits has played an important role in human life since early in mankind's history. So important has this role been, that neither church nor state has been able to suppress it.

References to divination existed in the Old Testament in the first book of Samuel in the Bible. King Saul orders all mediums and spiritualists expelled from Israel and requires the death penalty for anyone who dares conjure a spirit. But when he finds himself in need of advice and counsel from the late King Samuel he goes in disguise to the woman of Endor, a known medium who reluctantly conjures the spirit of Samuel. The name Endor means "fountain of Dor." The village is situated on a mountain that is riddled through with caves. Both caves and, as we shall soon see, fountains are associated with the evocation of spirits.

The spirit of Samuel apparently reveals the identity of Saul to the woman, because she suddenly shrieks and says to the king, "Why have you deceived me? You are Saul!"

Only after he assures the woman that no harm will befall her does she reveal the spirit of Samuel to Saul. Upon seeing the late king, Saul falls to the ground and addresses Samuel.

"I am in great distress," he says. "The Philistines are fighting against me, and God has turned away from me.

He no longer answers me, either by prophets or dreams. So I have called on you to tell me what to do."

Samuel replies with a horrifying prophecy that turns out to be true: "Why do you consult me now that the Lord has turned away from you and become your enemy? The Lord has done what he predicted through me. The Lord has torn the kingdom out of your hands and given it to one of your neighbors—to David. Because you did not obey the Lord or carry out his fierce wrath against the Amalekites the Lord will hand over both Israel and you to the Philistines and tomorrow you and your sons will be with me. The Lord will also hand over the army of Israel to the Philistines."

What sort of medium is the woman using to conjure the spirit of Samuel? Although the method she uses to call the spirit is not clearly spelled out in the Bible, she may be using some kind of speculum, a shiny object that could project a mirror image for visionary facilitation. It may be in the clear depth of such a reflection that King Saul's painful vision quest could take place.

A servant of Joseph referred to his using a silver cup as a gazing speculum when he said, "Is not this it in which my lord drinketh, and whereby he indeed divineth?" In a later verse Joseph sang praises of his talents when he said, "Know ye not that such a man as I can indeed divine?"

Anthropologists and others who have visited tribal cultures report methods similar to those in the Old Testament to consult the spirits.

SHAMANIC TRADITION

In Siberia, for instance, Tungus shamans used copper mirrors to "place the spirits." In their language the word for "mirror" was actually derived from the word for "soul" or "spirit," and hence the mirror was regarded as a receptacle for the spirit. These shamans claimed to be able to see the spirits of dead people by gazing into mirrors. The word *shaman*, by the way, originated with the Tungus tribe. The purpose of a shaman is to heal problems of daily life that occur either in the community or with individuals.

At one time the Malagasy of Madagascar evoked the spirits of the dead in the course of elaborate group ceremonies. Among these people it was customary to discuss the apparitions they had seen of their departed dear ones and also to discuss openly their interactions with these spirits. The shamans in the tribe would initiate such ceremonies by contacting spirits in mirrors.

As in the passage by Homer describing the visions of Odysseus, blood was used as a gazing medium by the Pawnee Indians of North America. Their method of mirror gazing was similar to that of the Greeks. When a member of the tribe killed a badger, it was kept by the older members of the tribe until night and then skinned. The blood was poured into a bowl, and the children had to look at their reflections in the moonlight. If they saw themselves with gray hair, it meant long life; if the picture was dark and indistinct, the child would die of sickness; if no picture was seen at all, the child would someday be killed by the enemy.

The Africans of Fez used a vessel of water in which to see visions. In present-day Egypt a pool of ink is used in much the same way that Odysseus uses blood. Dee Halde, a traveler who visited China in the early eighteenth century, recorded that the Tabist seers observed in a cauldron of water the events transpiring throughout the empire. The Zulus of Africa revered a chief's vessel that was used to make divinations after being filled with water. Shamans in northern equatorial Africa made medical diagnoses by gazing into a kettle of water.

One of the most intriguing uses of mirror gazing is that of the Nkomis tribe of Cap Lopez. They use mirror gazing in a manhood ritual that is conducted this way: After a long fast the initiate is confined to a hut. At one end of the hut stands a wooden statue. A packet of bones from someone long dead is placed beneath the statue. In front of the statue is a mirror.

The initiate is told to gaze into the mirror until he sees the face of a man. When he finally sees the face, he is asked to describe it. If he succeeds in describing the dead man whose bones are in the packet, he goes on to the next step in the manhood ritual.

In a recent book on the medicinal properties of plants, Richard Evans Schultes, and Albert Hoffman the chemist who discovered LSD, discuss a West African tribe that maintains contact with dead relatives using a plant and a mirror. The plant, called the *iboga*, is consumed in large quantities by people who then gaze into a mirror.

Members of the Bwiti tribe have told anthropologists

that the combination of plant and mirror "break open the head" so that their spirit can be carried away to "the land of the dead." One member of the tribe wrote a short poem about his experience that comes as close to explaining what happened as is verbally possible:

> I found myself taken by it up a long road
> in a deep forest,
> until I came to a barrier of black iron.
> At that barrier, unable to pass,
> I saw a crowd of black persons
> also unable to pass.
> In the distance . . . it was very bright.
> I could see many colors in the air . . .
> Suddenly my father descended from above
> in the form of a bird.
> He gave me then my Eboka name
> and enabled me to fly up after him
> over the barrier of iron.

ALADDIN'S MIRROR, NUMA'S NYMPHS

The theme of spirits being conjured from mirrors has also enlivened the literary imagination of cultures other than the Greeks. It is now clear to me that several of the *Arabian Nights* tales contain descriptions of mirror visions. For instance the story of Aladdin and his lamp is one of raising spirits. Unlike my work, the story does not deal with the souls of the departed but with spirits of another sort called genies. These ominous characters

61

were capable of granting wishes to the person lucky enough to rub them out of the lamps where they imprisoned.

The first to rub the lamp in the *Arabian Nights* tale is Aladdin's mother, who polishes the lamp with sand in order to shine it up so that she can sell it. In the process of doing this a gigantic genie appears who "was as horrifying as he was huge."

"Tell me what you want, mistress," he booms. "I am your slave and beholden to anyone who holds the lamp."

So frightened was Aladdin's mother that she begs her son, "by the milk with which I suckled you, throw away the lamp and the ring!"

It is plain that when Aladdin's mother polishes the metal lamp, she makes a reflective surface in which the genie can be seen as a mirror vision. Then the vision appears to actually leave the reflective surface and emerge into the physical world.

In bygone days metal lamps were used for divination, too, a practice that was called *lampadomancy*. I have an old brass whale-oil lamp from India, and I can see why such a tradition could get started. I have found that it makes an excellent speculum for mirror gazing when polished.

All of this leads me to believe that the idea for the genie that got out of the bottle most likely came from a mirror vision.

Beings called *nymphs* show up in Roman myth with the discussion of Numa, the second king of Rome. He, like all

Romans, had a belief in water fairies who emerged from the crystal-clear water of fountains.

It becomes quite clear that Egeria was a mirror being when we read Saint Augustine's comment. In *The City of God* he writes, "Numa himself, being not instructed by any prophet of God, was fain to fall to hydromancy; making his Gods (or rather his devils) to appear in water, and instruct him in his religious institutions."

CELTIC GAZING MYTH

A Celtic manuscript dating from the twelfth century tells of an adventure in the life of Lludd, an early king of Britain, in which cauldron gazing was used to capture troublesome dragons. These dragons emitted a scream so horrible that "the men lost their color and their strength and the women miscarried, and the boys and girls lost their minds, and all the animals and trees and the earth and the waters were left barren." These dragons posed a problem for the future of Lludd's domain, and he had to figure out a way to get rid of them. He consulted his brother, the king of France, who said that the dragons could be conjured up in a tub of honey wine and captured in a cloth of silk.

"Then you fold the cloth around them at once," said Lludd's brother, "and bury them in a stone chest and cover them up in the earth, in whatever place you may find to be the most secure in your kingdom."

Lludd did as suggested, covering the honey wine with the cloth of silk and gazing into it until visions of the dragons appeared. When eventually they were trapped in the silk, Lludd disposed of them.

The story of Lludd is a link in the continuing story of the cauldron, which shows up as a pivotal scene in Shakespeare's *Macbeth*, where three witches boil a hoary brew and conjure apparitions from its bubbling mist.

These are rituals in medieval sources for making spirits appear to divulge information otherwise unknown to the questioners. Young boys served as surrogate gazers and saw spirits that divulged information. Procedures for conjuring up spirits of the departed were sometimes included in collections of medical material, which raises the possibility that they were actually used by physicians. One wonders if this was even a form of grief counseling.

Some of these techniques show up in Goethe's great play on the legendary Dr. Faustus. Throughout the Faust legend methods for mirror gazing are revealed. There are mirror-gazing methods for discovering a thief, traveling out-of-body, diagnosing illness, and even one for summoning nine aerial spirits by gazing into a glass filled with spring water.

A real-life Dr. Faustus of sorts lived in the eighteenth century in the form of Count Cagliostro. He created an international sensation when he taught people how to gaze into reflective surfaces and see images. One writer wrote about Cagliostro's spirit and how it appeared and conversed with him in "crystals and under glass bells."

A GAZER CALLED 007

Perhaps the most fascinating story of conjuring is that of John Dee, a noted scholar and innovator from Elizabethan England. Born in 1527, he vowed to devote his life to learning, and he studied all day, every day, throughout his teenage years. His devotion to study paid off. By the time he was in his early twenties, he was a lecturer at many universities, especially in France, where his eccentricities were appreciated.

He was also an accomplished inventor whose work sometimes got him into trouble. When his students staged one of Aristophanes' comedies, Dee decided to enhance the production by building a special-effects apparatus—a giant bug that actually appeared to fly.

The bug amused most of the people who saw it and even frightened some. The superstitious in the audience would leap to their feet and shout, "Sorcerer!" when the device operated.

Charges of witchcraft followed him all his life. Once he even grew so impatient with the persecution that he asked to be tried just to settle the matter once and for all. As he wrote in his petition to the king, such a trial would confound those "Brainsicke, Rashe, Spitefull, and Disdainful Countrey men" who were making his life so miserable. He even said he would gladly be stoned if such a charge as sorcerer or "invocator of devils" could be proven.

He became an internationally recognized scholar in his twenties and was an expert in navigational techniques and equipment. He wrote one of the standard textbooks of mathematics and invented a device that helped sailors read maps.

He was an associate of Queen Elizabeth, for whom he worked as a sort of private intelligence agent. She was said to be fascinated by Dee's eyes and nicknamed him "Eyes." Accordingly, when he signed his secret communications to her, he did so by drawing two circles side by side to represent eyes and made a mark over and beside the two circles that resembled a figure seven, perhaps to signal his appreciation of the lucky number. The resulting signature was one that looked like 007, the code name for James Bond, the modern-day spy who also served in Her Majesty's secret service.

While studying artifacts brought from Mexico by Spaniards, Dee discovered an obsidian divination mirror that was apparently used by the Aztecs. He was surprised to find that he could see visions in it and soon began using this discovery in his work with the queen. She even went to his house one day to see this extraordinary speculum.

His dwelling was in fact a combination museum, library, and consciousness-research center, where he maintained a variety of curiosities and one of the finest collections of books in the land. Despite his royal connections and high standing in the academic world, he was still regarded as a sorcerer by London's uneducated masses. These superstitious people were at one time incited to riot against Dee by jealous members of the queen's court. They attacked and burned his home while he was traveling abroad. One account of this event says that Dee watched his books burn from afar, seeing images of it in his obsidian mirror. The account says he accepted it stoically, since there was nothing he could do about it.

In the home that was destroyed Dee had set aside a chamber in which to have mirror visions. He laboriously recorded these visions in a detailed and lengthy manuscript, only a portion of which survives. In these writings he describes spirits who appear first in the speculum and then actually emerge as if in the chamber.

One of these spirits, a young woman named Madimi, showed up regularly and actually seemed to walk around the room. Dee also records that these beings spoke and apparently even carried on conversations with him. For example, one of these beings, called angels by Dee, gave him this bit of whole-earth wisdom: "Ignorance was the nakedness wherewithal you were first tormented, and the first Plague that fell unto man was the want of Science; . . . the want of Science hindreth you from knowledge of yourself."

Scholars have long set aside Dee's reports, dismissing them as impossible, but I think that he was conjuring wisdom and beings from the depths of the unconscious mind.

Dee didn't think he was doing that, though. The great scientist was employing everything in his power to reach God. He hoped that through communication with the angels he could reunite Catholics and Protestants under one Christian belief, that of universal love. Despite warnings from the leaders of both churches that he was close to being tried as a heretic, Dee continued to publicize his communications with angels.

Dee's belief that he was talking to angels through his obsidian mirror did him no good in the royal court. James I had succeeded Elizabeth in 1603, and he was very sensitive to anything that smacked of witchcraft. Since Dee had been such a loyal servant of Queen Elizabeth's, the new king ignored the charges of conjuring that some members of the clergy wanted brought against him, but he banished Dee from the royal court.

Ostracized by his fellow scientists, Dee died in 1608. His final days were passed in the care of his daughter, who was at times forced to sell his precious books to raise money for food.

After he died, a carefully prepared manuscript of his works on mirror gazing disappeared for decades. It reemerged in the shop of a London fishmonger, who was using its pages to wrap fish. The enitre manuscript might have been lost forever had it not been discovered by an academic who happened to read the wrappings of his fish.

PRESIDENTIAL MIRROR VISION

An American president, too, has found illumination through mirror visions. On the night of the fateful election of 1860, Abraham Lincoln reclined, exhausted, on the couch. Suddenly, in a nearby mirror, he saw a strange double image of himself, one image as he was and one that looked pale and ghostly.

Lincoln told his wife, Mary, of this experience. The

First Lady interpreted the vision this way: She said that he would be elected to a second term but then would die in office. His mirror vision and her interpretation proved to be prophetic.

It is surprising, given the universality of the wish for reunion with the dearly departed, that mirror-gazing skills have almost disappeared. One reason seems to be that practitioners have maintained professional secrecy about their techniques.

The fact that fumigation and a ritual bath followed the evocation at Ephyra implies that the facilitators, whoever they were knew that "processing" rituals were needed to ease the apparition seekers back into reality. The woman of Endor's touching gesture of feeding Saul before he left shows that she, too, understood the need to be comforted after these experiences.

There has also been religious suppression. Religious organizations with rigid ideologies have an interest in discouraging people from seeking firsthand experience in the spiritual realm. Since the practice of mirror gazing gives people access to their spiritual universe, the leaders of various religions (not just Christianity but many other state religions as well) drove this practice underground. Many religions showed their loving concern for humanity by burning such offenders at the stake or otherwise eliminating them.

It is important to note that society has always dealt harshly with those who disturb consensus. Few principles of human life, whether cognitive or social, are more sacrosanct than the notion that there is an unbridgeable gap between the world of the living and the realm of the dead. Those who trespass across that boundary invite the strictest scrutiny.

FALSE HISTORY

It is highly likely that some falsehoods were recorded as fact and disseminated to keep people away from places that conjured the spirits of the dead. Or, perhaps, would-be facilitators couldn't figure out the techniques and attempted to fake it. There is a hint of this in one passage from the works of Hippolytus, a second-century bishop of Rome, who wrote to condemn the various occult "heresies":

> But neither shall I be silent respecting that piece of knavery of these sorcerers, which consists in the divination by means of the cauldron. For making a closed chamber, and anointing the ceiling with cyanus [a dark blue paint] for present use, they introduce certain vessels of cyanus, and stretch them upwards. The cauldron, however, full of water, is placed in the middle of the ground, and the reflection of the cyanus falling upon it, presents the appearance of heaven. But the floor also has a certain concealed aperture, on which the cauldron is laid, having been previously supplied with a bottom of crystal, while itself is composed of stone. Underneath, however, unnoticed by the spectators,

is a compartment, into which the accomplices assembling, appear invested with the figures of such gods and demons as the magician wishes to exhibit.

There are many reasons that some people—particularly those in institutions or professions—would like to suppress mirror gazing. The reasons range from fundamentalist fervor to fear of superstition.

I don't pretend to imply that all who mirror-gaze have been honest souls with only good intentions. There have been as many frauds in this field as there have been in any other, from the medical profession to plumbing.

Should we discount something useful because a few people abuse it or because it goes against the mainstream? I don't think we should. History has shown the value of mirror gazing as well as its blemishes. It has also shown the willingness of some to fight for what they believe in.

The defiant and stoic John Dee comes to mind. He challenged the citizens of England to try him for witchcraft. He was even imprisoned for six months for the "lewde vayne practices of conjuring." Still he continued to spend time gazing into his obsidian mirror, bravely writing down accounts of the spirits he encountered in its clear depth.

One might wonder why such a major intellectual force in Elizabethan England would risk his reputation in this way. Didn't it make his life far more difficult? Indeed it did. But he sought total knowledge and wanted to know as much about himself and the world around him as he could. Ridicule obviously meant little to a man who wrote in his diaries, "I may and must professe in the first place, in Truth and Sincerity, that the end that I propose to my self is not to satisfie curiosity, but to do good."

THREE

A MODERN-DAY PSYCHOMANTEUM

Those who dream by day are cognizant of many things which escape those who dream only by night
—Edgar Allan Poe

After researching the role of mirror gazing through history, I decided to attempt to facilitate visionary encounters with the departed in much the way the Greeks had.

I conceived a procedure by which, I believed, apparitions of the dead could be evoked among living people. But would it be safe to actually carry out such a procedure? I consulted Dr. William Roll, one of the leading experts on apparitions of the deceased, who informed me that he had never once uncovered a case in which harm had come to anyone from an apparition. In fact, unlike the popular image portrayed in horror films and books, he found these experiences to be beneficial in that they alleviate grief or even bring about its resolution.

First there needed to be a special kind of environment

in which the procedure could be carried out. To provide such an environment, I converted the upstairs of my old gristmill in Alabama to a modern-day psychomanteum. Mine was a modernized version of the ones found in ancient Greece, with the same goal in mind, that of seeing apparitions of the departed.

A room was set aside for use as an apparition chamber. At one end of the room a mirror four feet tall and three and a half feet wide was mounted on the wall. The bottom edge of the mirror was three feet above the floor.

A comfortable easy chair was prepared by removing its legs so that the top of the headrest was about three feet above the floor. The chair was placed about three feet from the mirror and inclined slightly backward. This was done for comfort but also to keep the reflection of the gazer from being seen in the mirror. In effect the angle of the chair created a clear depth view of the mirror, which would reflect only the darkness behind the person who was gazing. The result was a crystal-clear pool of darkness.

This pool of darkness was assured by the black velvet curtain draped all around the chair from the ceiling. A curved curtain rod was used to allow the drape to surround the area around the chair and mirror, creating a curtained booth or chamber. Inside this apparition chamber and directly behind the chair was placed a small stained-glass lamp with a fifteen-watt bulb. When the lights in the room were turned off and the outside light excluded by blinds and thick window curtains, this tiny light provided the room's only illumination.

This simple room, with its dim light, darkened

surroundings, and the clear depth of the mirror provided the ideal mirror-gazing environment. I was now ready to test my theories.

THE INITIAL STUDY

The question posed initially was a simple one: Can apparitions of deceased loved ones be consistently facilitated in normal, healthy people? To examine this simple question, I assembled ten test subjects who were willing to devote the time necessary to the experiment.

As with most studies of this nature, I had criteria for the test subjects:

- They must be mature people interested in human consciousness.
- They must be emotionally stable, inquisitive, and articulate.
- None of the subjects could have emotional or mental disorders, to lessen the likelihood that the procedure would cause a bad reaction.
- None of the subjects could have occult ideologies, since such leanings could complicate the analysis of the results.

I contacted a number of people known to me who fitted these criteria. Included were counselors, psychologists, medical doctors, graduate students. and professionals in other fields.

The project was explained in detail to all the subjects.

What we were trying to do, I told them, was to evoke an apparition of a deceased person to whom they had been close and whom they would like to see again. They were then asked to select a few mementos, objects that had been owned by the deceased person and were strongly and poignantly associated with them. They would bring these objects with them to the psychomanteum on the day of their apparitional facilitation.

I then scheduled their sessions, making certain to deal with only one subject at a time. Each of the subjects was asked to arrive at ten A.M. on the appointed day and to bring the mementos and even photo albums if they were available. They were also asked to dress in loose-fitting clothing and comfortable walking shoes. A light breakfast beforehand was okay.

Upon arriving the subject and I took a leisurely walk in the countryside. On these strolls we explored the person's motivation for attempting to see the departed. The subject was told that there was no guarantee that an apparition would be seen. This of course was true. There was no way I could promise that an apparition *would* be seen, but my other reason for doing this was more subtle. I wanted to remove any pressure to have an experience. Such pressure could cause anxiety and reduce the chances of having an apparitional experience.

After the walk we ate a light lunch of soup, salad, fruit, and fruit juice or decaffeinated soda. Then we sat down for a lengthy talk, during which time we discussed in detail the person who had died and the relationship that had existed between the two of them. We explored such areas as the type of person the deceased had been, his or her appearance, habits—virtually every aspect of personality.

Usually the subject would bring up important and touching memories. Throughout our conversation the mementos were right there between us and were frequently handled by the subject. Some of these mementos were quite touching. One man brought his father's fishing equipment. A woman brought her sister's hat. These objects functioned as poignant and tangible reminders of the deceased.

Before some of the subjects entered the apparition chamber, I had them lie on a bed built by one of my staff members. A comfortable recliner equipped with speakers, the bed induces a profound state of relaxation with music that permeates the subject's body through bone conduction. I used this bed with maybe half of the subjects in order to deepen their level of relaxation.

These preparatory sessions lasted until dusk. Then the subject was escorted into the mirror-gazing booth, the lamp inside was turned on, and all the remaining light in the room was extinguished. The subject was then told to gaze deeply into the mirror and to relax, clearing his or her mind of everything but thoughts of the deceased person. The subject could stay in the chamber as long as he wanted, but was asked not to wear a watch so that he would not be tempted to glance at the time.

An attendant sat in the next room during the entire session, prepared to render any assistance needed. When the subject emerged, an extended processing session was conducted, during which the subject discussed what had happened. She was allowed to ventilate feelings and discuss the entire experience until she felt there was nothing more to discuss. Sometimes these de-briefing sessions would go on for more than an hour, I made it a point not to interfere or to hurry them along. The session wasn't over until *the subject* decided it was over.

"WHAT I SAW WAS THE REAL PERSON"

A typical case was a man who wanted to see his late mother. He came to me after hearing a talk I gave in New Jersey in which I discussed the possibilities of mirror gazing.

He told me that his mother had passed away the previous year and that he missed her greatly. His father had died when he was young, leaving his mother to care for him. As a result he formed an unusually strong attachment to her and had grieved deeply since her death.

I probed into his personal history. He was in his mid-forties and was in a high-level position at a certified public accounting firm in New York City. He had never been treated for any sort of psychological problems.

I thought he would be an excellent subject for the research project. Not only was he a willing subject able to understand the process, but he fitted the criteria for being in the study that I have outlined.

I was excited when he asked to fly down and spend a day with me. When he arrived for his session we followed the protocol that I outlined above. In the morning we took a long walk in the country and talked about his motivations for wanting to see his late mother. I have always found exercise to be a tremendously effective means of freeing up a person's thoughts. There are even some psychologists who make walking and running a part of their regular method of therapy. So it was with this subject. As we walked, he began to tell stories about his mother. And as he told stories of her sacrifices as a single mother, he was clearly moved by the remembrances.

"She was very sick at the end of her life," he said. "I guess that one of the reasons I want to see her again is to make sure she is happy wherever she is."

After lunch we looked through photo albums with picture after picture of him and his mother as they had aged over the years. The early pictures revealed a robust and happy woman, but the photos at the end of the album showed a woman ravaged by age and illness. In some of them the face of this man was pressed close to his mother's. Although he was smiling, it was clear from the pictures that his mother's failing condition was wearing heavily on his emotions.

We examined the mementos he had brought. There was a sweater she had worn later in life, along with a hat she had worn when she was young.

"Clothing has memory," he said, explaining these particular mementos. "I wanted to bring something along that would remind me of how she felt and even how she moved."

In the evening I took this man into the apparition

chamber and explained the procedure to him. Then I left him alone. Nearly an hour later he emerged. He wore a broad smile on his face and had tears running down his cheeks. He was elated at what had happened, he said. We sat down in my office where he told me what he had seen:

There is no doubt that the person I saw in the mirror was my mother! I don't know where she came from, but I am convinced that what I saw was the real person. She was looking out at me from the mirror. I couldn't tell what clothing she was wearing, but I could tell that she was in her later seventies, about the same age as she was when she died. However, she looked healthier and happier than she had at the end of her life.

Her lips didn't move, but she spoke to me, and I clearly heard what she had to say. She said, "I'm fine," and smiled happily.

I stayed as relaxed as I could and just looked at her. My hands were tingling, and I could feel my heartbeat pick up speed. Then I decided to talk to her. I said, "It's good to see you again." "It's good to see you too," she replied. That was it. She simply disappeared.

The experience made him relax about his mother's death. "Just from what I saw and heard, I can see that she is no longer in pain like she was in her last days," he said. "That alone removes a lot of stress from my life."

The subject was sure that his mother was truly in that

mirror, but he was not prepared to say where the image of her came from. It may have been some form of memory, or it may truly have been the spirit body of his mother, he said. But whatever the answer was, he was not able to deliver it. "I don't know exactly what caused it, but I do know that I saw my mother."

SURPRISING RESULTS

Even before a single subject had been guided through a mirror-gazing session, I assumed that only a small percentage of the subjects—maybe one out of the ten— would experience an apparition. I also believed all the subjects would be dubious about the "reality" of the encounter and would be unsure if what had happened was "real" or just "in their minds."

The picture that emerged from the experience, however, is dramatically different from what I initially imagined. After conducting just ten people through the process of visionary facilitation, I realized it was possible to duplicate the common human experience of seeing apparitions of the deceased. Of the ten I ushered through the process, five saw apparitions of their departed relatives. Later, after improving my facilities and refining my technique, I conducted visionary facilitations with even better results. Still I look back at that early research and marvel at those first case studies.

"LET MY MOTHER KNOW THAT I AM FINE"

One of my favorite subjects from these early cases was a physician from the West Coast who came to have a reunion with his late aunt. Instead, an unexpected reunion took place with his departed nephew. The encounter left him in an awkward position. Although this was just an auditory experience, it left the subject firmly convinced that he had spoken to the young boy. Here is his story in his words:

I had not really been planning to meet up with my nephew while I was there in the apparition room. I sat there for what seemed like a long period of time. As I was sitting there trying to force a vision, nothing was coming up of any significance. All of a sudden I stopped forcing it and just sat back and relaxed. I was figuring, "Well, I'm not going to be able to have my apparition."

That is when I suddenly had a very strong sense of the presence of my nephew, who had committed suicide. I was close to this nephew, who was named after my father and me.

There was this very strong sense of his presence, and I heard his voice very clearly. He was talking to me. He greeted me and he brought me a very simple message: He said, "Let my mother know that I am fine and that I love her very much."

This experience was very profound, I know he

was there with me. I didn't see anything, but I had a very strong sense of him and of his presence. This voice is different from just having a thought and it is not exactly like the regular experience of hearing a voice. It is like being spoken to mentally. I cannot say exactly what it is, but I can say what it is not. It is a form of communication. I feel sure that I was in communication with my nephew.

This visionary encounter presented an interpersonal dilemma to the physician. He felt completely confident that he had actually been in the presence of his departed nephew. He also felt an obligation to do as he had agreed to do, which was pass his nephew's message on to his sister. He was unsure how his sister would react to this news and whether she would think that he had lost his mind.

He told me that he had tentatively decided to broach the subject by telling his sister that he had had an extremely vivid dream. When I spoke with him eight months later, he had decided to tell his sister the truth about how the encounter had come about. She proved to be very understanding about her brother's experience.

"HE WAS HUGGING ME"

A woman came to see her late grandfather. She brought a photo album and openly discussed her love for him as she thumbed through the pages of pictures. Although she went into the mirror booth fully expecting to see her grandfather, neither one of us was prepared for what happened. Not only did she see and talk to her grandfather, but he also came out of the mirror and comforted her when she began to cry at seeing him again.

I was so happy to see him that I began to cry. Through the tears I could still see him in the mirror. Then he seemed to get closer and he must have come out of the mirror because the next thing I knew he was holding me and hugging me. It felt like he said something like, "It's okay, don't cry."

Before I knew it, he was gone. I can still feel his touch. I also feel warm, like someone has been hugging me.

It was great to see him again. He was happy and that's good. Even though I miss him it's nice to know that he's happy where he is.

That she would actually feel her grandfather's embrace surprised me, even though tactile encounters with ghosts are quite common in the parapsychology research. In one study 13 percent of the contacts with the dead were of the tactile variety, which means that a person felt the ghost. Typical of these are widows who feel their deceased husbands, often when lying in bed at night or in the morning. Although I was familiar with the research on "feeling" ghosts in the scientific literature, I didn't expect it to happen with the participants of this study. It happened not only to this subject but to others as well.

"YOU ARE LIVING THE RIGHT WAY"

An example of an auditory vision comes from a South American woman who came to the psychomanteum in hopes of seeing an apparition of her late husband. He had been in his early forties when he died the previous year of a heart attack.

The morning of his death he had admitted himself into the hospital with severe chest pains. The doctors had conducted a number of standard medical tests on him but could find nothing wrong with his heart. Late in the day they had discharged him and he went home. A few hours later as he and his family were preparing to eat dinner, he clutched his chest and fell dead on the floor.

The wife was not prepared for the loss of her husband. She suddenly found herself the sole provider for four children.

We discussed just what it was she hoped to get out of the visionary facilitation. Her main concern, she said, was to make sure that her husband was all right in the afterlife. She also wanted to know if he approved of the way she was conducting the family's business. Her life had become extremely hectic in that she seemed to be working constantly to fulfill all of the roles of a widowed parent. Stress wrinkled her face as she talked about life without her husband.

"I never know if I am doing the right things but I can't slow down to think about it," she said. "I also can't relax. I have been to counselors and doctors, but they haven't been able to put me at ease."

After going through the standard procedures, I led this subject to the apparitional chamber. Here, in her own words, is what happened:

I saw many clouds and lights and movement from one side of the mirror to the other. There were lights in the clouds that were changing colors also. For a moment I thought I was going to see him. But it didn't happen that way.

Instead I suddenly felt his presence. I didn't see him, but I knew he was standing right next to me. Then I heard him speak. He told me, "Go ahead, you are living the right way and you are raising the kids the right way."

Then we began to see things in the crystal from our life together. We re-experienced them. For instance, I could see us in the delivery room when he was there with me for the birth of one of our children. I had been so glad to have him there when that happened, and it was as though we were living it over again. I saw many other things we had done together, and I was as happy looking at them now as I had been with him.

Was I frightened? I was not frightened at all. On the contrary I was more relaxed than I have been since he died. I knew nothing bad was going to happen there. I was with my husband, how could anything bad happen?

I have felt that he was with us all this last year. I know he died because I saw him, but I really felt that he was with us. But I have never experienced his presence like I did here. We were experiencing the same things as when he was alive.

Now I want to follow this experience with another one. I feel him closer, and I want to nudge it with another time in the apparition booth to see if I can actually see him.

The next day this subject tried the visionary facilitation again. She was even more relaxed with the techniques, and the results were far better than the previous day's. This time she could actually hear her husband speaking to her in a clear voice. Although she didn't actually see him, she could feel him standing next to her.

I saw more of our life together, but today it was different. I saw some flashes of him in the mirror, but I heard him very clearly talking to me. It was as though he was there in the room, and as I thought questions, he answered them.

He felt sorry for me that my life was so hard. But he said it was what I had to do now and that I shouldn't really take life so hard.

I was so glad. I wanted to hold him, but I knew that was impossible. Still it was wonderful to know that he is with us when we need him.

The subject was immediately relieved by both of these experiences. Much of the stress that had furrowed her face before the mirror gazing was now gone. She smiled happily after the sessions where before she did not smile at all.

In her case the visionary facilitation did two things. It reassured her that her husband was no longer in pain but was instead quite enthusiastic about where he was. "I know he is fine," she said. "He has told me he is fine through this experience." It was important for her to know this, especially since he had died such a sudden and painful death. This experience fulfilled the need she'd had for her husband's life to have a happy ending.

The contact with her husband also served to confirm that she was doing the right things as a mother. Since the death of her husband this woman had taken two jobs in addition to the very full-time position of raising four children. She was performing this awesome task of single-parenting and was always wondering if what she was doing as a mother would meet with her husband's approval. Now she had that approval. In each of the mirror-gazing sessions her husband had expressed his belief that she was raising their children the best she could and in a way of which he approved.

"I can now be sure of things that I wasn't before," she told me. "I am now convinced that he is with me. He is trying to help me at every moment."

The subject left the psychomanteum feeling greatly relieved. In many ways the painful last year had come full circle. She was now relaxed and confident, ready to face the future. "Now I have confirmation and I feel as though I can go on and live my life with another vision of the future," she said. "I don't have to worry anymore."

"I AM FINE AND I LOVE YOU"

Another subject, a surgeon from a city in the East, sought reunion with his mother, who had died in 1968. He felt he owed his mother a great debt of gratitude for his personal success. He had missed her greatly over the years and frequently wondered what his life would be like if his mother were still alive. With a desire just to see his mother again, this man went into the apparition booth. He emerged with this story:

> I went into the booth a little bit apprehensive, not particularly sure that this was going to work for me. I sat there for a long time, trying to disengage my mind and get into the appropriate state. Finally I got so relaxed that I think I started to doze off.
>
> At this point, as I gazed into the mirror a sort of filmy, smoky substance came across the glass. Then out of this mist there was a figure forming and sitting on a sofa of some sort.
>
> At first I just saw the outline of the form and didn't see any details. Then, further on, maybe a minute later, the form started to show some features. And they all didn't appear at once. They were more like the computerized pictures you see on television. The face sort of filled in from the top down, and after a while, I said, 'That's my mother."

"How are you?" I asked.

Her lips didn't move, but I got a mental communication from her in which she said, "I'm fine and I love you."

I asked her another question: "Was there any pain when you died?"

"None at all," I could hear her say. "The transition to death was easy."

At first I verbalized my questions, just said them right out loud. But before I got a few of the questions out, the answer would come back to me in a mental form. There was no sound of her speaking, I just knew what she was saying.

I asked her more questions, just by thinking them. "What do you think of the woman I plan to marry?" I asked.

"It will be a very good choice," she answered. "You should continue to work hard at the relationship and not be your old self. Try to be more understanding."

This lasted for maybe ten questions, and then she faded away and I couldn't talk to her anymore. I tried hard to bring her back, but there was so much emotion there that I couldn't do it. By the time it was over, I was extremely moved.

STUNNED BY THE RESULTS

These first cases stunned me. Although millions of people see visions of departed loved ones each year, scientists have always held that these apparitions occur spontaneously and cannot be made to happen. Visionary encounters happen when they happen, claim most researchers, and cannot be facilitated.

I had thought that this was true, but still I had my doubts. Now I had made them take place in a clinical setting.

Like the ancient Greeks, I had designed a psychomanteum, to which people could come to consult with the spirits of the deceased. It was clear that given the proper preparation, people could see apparitions of departed loved ones using these techniques.

I found this to be an exciting and useful notion. People who are saddened by the loss of a loved one could handle their grief in a more direct way. Instead of telling a therapist how they feel about losing a spouse or child, they could talk to the loved one directly.

Through my work in near-death studies I know that seeing departed loved ones is tremendously therapeutic. Encountering dead relatives is one element of the near-death experience that keeps it from being a frightening or traumatic event. Research has shown that near-death experiences transform people's lives by making them less fearful of death. One reason they become less fearful is that they see that dead relatives are happy in the afterlife.

Grief resolution results from both seeing an apparition and having a near-death experience, and this is one way these two experiences are alike. Visionary encounters with departed loved ones are not frightening. On the contrary, they tend to be positive experiences that give people hope and a sense that the departed is comfortable, happy, and still with them spiritually.

For example, a man in Pennsylvania lost his favorite daughter in an accident. She had gone swimming at a lake with several friends and drowned. The man went to the lake and waited stoically on the shore until divers brought her body to the surface. Then he accompanied his daughter's body to the mortuary and made all the arrangements for her funeral.

Two days later, on the day of the burial services, the man was putting his tie on in front of the bathroom mirror when an apparition of the dead daughter suddenly appeared next to him. She was still dressed in her swimsuit and was soaking wet as though she had just been pulled out of the lake. She stood next to her father and put her hand on his shoulder. Then she kissed him on the cheek, said, "Good-bye," and disappeared.

This story was told to me by this man's other daughter, who insisted that his shoulder and the side of his face were wet when he came out of the bathroom and told his family of his remarkable experience.

"He told that story until the day he died," said the woman. "People asked him if it gave him the creeps, but it didn't. He was very comforted at seeing her one more time."

Excited by the possibilities that mirror gazing presented, I decided to press on with further research.

FOUR

THE THEATER OF THE MIND

Explore what you are scoffed at for wanting to explore.

—Source unknown

In the spring of 1990, having realized that I needed a special space in which to conduct further investigations into mirror gazing, I decided, as I mentioned before, to convert my old mill house into an appropriate facility. I called it the Theater of the Mind. At the theater a variety of elements—art, music, play, relaxation, creative activity, physical exercise, nature, hypnagogic states, perceptual illusions, intellectual stimulation, and humor —have been combined to create an atmosphere that is naturally conducive to the creation of altered states of consciousness.

The theater is so multifaceted that it is at once a temple, a fortune-teller's parlor, a spiritual retreat center, an art museum, a school, a library, and a fun house. In addition, it resurrects some of the long-forgotten

93

institutions of the ancient world, such as the Greek oracles of the dead; the dream-incubation temples of Asklepios; and the *Museion*, the forerunner to our own museums, where people went to seek inspiration from the Muses. All of this was combined in such a way as to create an environment in which visionary encounters could occur.

FACTORS THAT ENABLE ALTERED STATES

My strategy has been to incorporate as many of the factors that are known to ease one's transition into altered states of reality as possible. The overall purposes of the Theater of the Mind are education, entertainment, spiritual growth, and grief therapy through altered states of awareness. The following factors contribute to attaining these altered states of consciousness:

The Beauty of Nature
The wonders of nature can cause mystical and other spiritual experiences. Something deep within human beings is very powerfully moved by natural beauty.

To provide a potent burst of contact with nature, the Theater of the Mind is housed in a former gristmill beside a creek in a secluded rural area of Alabama. Numerous wild creatures roam the creek banks outside the living-room windows, and the thick green forest provides seclusion from civilization and enables clients to take walks and commune with nature during their stay.

Alterations in the Sense of Time

People who experience altered states of consciousness often report that their sense of time is distorted during these episodes. To help subjects become *lost* in time, I ask them not to wear watches. I am also careful to make sure that no clocks are in sight. Sometimes I set up a sundial in the yard as a subtle reminder of a more primitive method of reckoning time.

Not only are the timepieces anachronistic, but so is the decor. Antique furniture is used throughout, and an extensive library of nineteenth-century stereoscopic cards provides a kind of window into a time long past.

All of this combined with the mill itself, which was built in 1839, have the effect of disorienting the conscious and subconscious mind and of propelling one back to an earlier era.

Subjects report a feeling of living in the past. Some say that it is as though they have been lifted out of the age of technology by a time machine that sent them back a hundred years.

Art and the Altered State

Art of all kinds can induce altered states. An Italian psychiatrist has identified what she calls the Stendahl syndrome. This bizarre affliction is akin to a nervous breakdown and takes place when people are exposed to great works of art. Stendahl syndrome is most frequently observed in Florence, Italy, and afflicts primarily tourists from countries with a strong work ethic. When they finally get to Florence, they are overcome by emotions when they see that city's great works of art. Some have what amounts to a mini nervous breakdown. After a few days of medical treatment the tourists recover. It is clear that the beauty of art seen after the sensory deprivation of hard work causes some kind of overload of the brain to take place.

Altered states of reality have also been chronicled among musicians by concert pianist Erik Pigani. A number of renowned performing artists he has personally interviewed have undergone profound spiritual experiences while performing great musical masterpieces. Some have reported the sensation of being bathed in light.

Pigani himself became interested in altered states among musicians when he had an out-of-body experience during a concert and suddenly found himself floating above the stage watching his own performance.

All of this makes me believe that art and music stimulate many altered states of consciousness, such as out-of-body experiences.

Through the use of art an effort has been made to contribute to alerted states at the Theater of the Mind. Provocative and unusual paintings and drawings are displayed throughout the building. Art books are placed prominently in waiting areas, where subjects are encouraged to peruse them.

Art and decorations have been chosen not solely for their beauty but also to induce surprise, shock, or feelings of incongruity. Generally things are not matched in the theater, since matching items provide a sense of sameness, stability, and predictability. For example, each piece of china used during a meal is different. A plate may be a simple piece of bone china, while a ceramic cup will resemble a bundle of large blue grapes. In the living room a tall wooden Indian stands next to a Tiffany lamp. Pictures range from Maxfield Parrish posters of angels to classic scenes from Donald Duck cartoons. All of this has the effect of keeping the subject's mind preoccupied with novel stimuli and in a constant state of wonder.

Stimulation Through Knowledge and Humor

I keep an extensive library of books and related material on altered states of consciousness, the paranormal, and spirituality. Since knowledge has been an important channel through which people have sought spiritual direction and enlightenment, I encourage subjects to browse through the books.

I am careful to keep the intellectual aspects of our program from outweighing the fun. Humor, after all, is strongly associated with creativity. Mirth itself might well be classified as an altered state of consciousness, since the delightful feelings it brings have an intoxicating effect and directly relax the skeletal muscles of the body.

The incongruities of humor often lead to new insights and even self-understanding. Humor also serves to keep the subject relaxed about the experience ahead, that of seeing a departed loved one.

Creating a Sense of Play

Some people see play as a stage we go through on the way to becoming adults. Many adults have forgotten how to play and instead have developed a serious-minded approach to life.

Such people often have difficulty in entering altered states of awareness. They fail to see that there is a distinct link between play and the paranormal. Yet I have found that parapsychology and the paranormal are related at least as strongly to the realms of play, humor, and entertainment as they are to the realm of scientific inquiry.

In making this claim I don't intend to denigrate or ridicule parapsychology. In fact, by accepting this concept, I think a lot could be *added* to the study of parapsychology. Despite the tendency of certain dour types to downplay their importance, humor, play, and entertainment are among the most significant of human enterprises. In addition, creative play is one important wellspring of discovery.

In my opinion, to proclaim parapsychology's interconnections with entertainment liberates the field in a new way, potentially enabling it more elegantly to fulfill a valuable role in human affairs. Various works of art, which are forms of entertainment after all—whether poetry, music, painting, sculpture, or dramas—have long served to clarify or even advance the spiritual life of humankind.

In effect parapsychology is a systematic inquiry into the paranormal. Parapsychology, like art, can have a powerful and uplifting effect, stirring profound emotions of awe, amazement, hope, and wonder and helping us regain an appreciation of the uncanny nature of the universe in which we live.

The unconscious recognition that the examination of

the paranormal is fun might explain why fundamentalists disdain this field of study. After all, things that smack of play or humor are not their forte.

Because of my belief that play is linked strongly with the paranormal, I have introduced it in subtle ways into the mirror-gazing process. In the living room where the initial "get acquainted" session takes place, the subjects sit in large hammock-style chairs that are suspended from the ceiling. If they don't feel comfortable in those, subjects can sit on beanbag cushions that are scattered around on the floor.

Toys that appeal to adults as well as to children are always within arm's reach. These include kaleidoscopes, puzzles, magic tricks, colorful picture books, and a variety of other toys.

Mirrors are also located at prominent places throughout the building to symbolize the quest for self-understanding. At the same time, mirrors are a frequent focus of superstition, hence their presence sets up reverberations in a primitive level of the mind.

Gazing into a mirror can provide an opportunity for soul-searching and self-understanding. I have several normal mirrors scattered around as well as a set of funhouse mirrors that allow clients to experience distortion of body image, further loosening their attachment to the ordinary view of reality.

GATEWAY TO THE PSYCHE

The intended effect of these various elements is not to coerce participants into an attitude of frivolity or hilarity but to create a doorway into their own psyche, allowing them to explore other dimensions of their minds by safely surrendering some of their longest-held inhibitions. As one subject said in describing his experience, "It was like stepping through some kind of time barrier and into another world. It made me feel as though time were unreal."

The establishment of the Theater of the Mind, with its emphasis on art, antiques, nature, fun, and play, improved not only the quantity of apparitions people had but their quality as well. This increased success made me aware of the powerful role that mood can play in medicine, especially in that fuzzy area known as human psychology.

In the case of mirror gazing, the proper mood is established by the environment in which it is done. This environment can be considered ritualistic in that it sets up a pattern of behavior that leads to profound relaxation.

It is only after this relaxation is achieved that the subject is taken to the apparition chamber, where he or she gazes into the mirror where the visions take place.

I have been conducting mirror-gazing research at the Theater of the Mind since 1990. In that course of time I have directly observed several hundred individuals as they were mirror gazing and afterward interviewed them about the experience.

Many of these gazings were done for the purpose of having a facilitated vision of a departed loved one, which is the main focus of this book. Others were done to help people pursue self-understanding as part of a process of innovative psychotherapy.

These other uses for mirror gazing are discussed later in the book. For now I will confine myself to reporting some of the more surprising findings that relate to reunions with departed relatives.

Many subjects encounter a deceased person other than the one they prepared to see All of the subjects prepared to see a specific person. Yet approximately one fourth of the subjects saw a *different* deceased relative.

Apparitions were not confined to the mirror In about ten percent of the cases the apparitions seemed to come *out* of the mirror and into the surrounding environment. Subjects would often report that they were "touched" by the apparition or that they could feel them standing next to them. I should have expected this phenomenon to happen, since Dr. Dee writes about apparitions emerging from his mirror in the original accounts of his gazing experiments. In one case, however, an apparition of a departed person expressly forbade the subject to touch her.

The flip side of this scenario also took place. About ten percent of the subjects reported taking journeys *into* the looking glass, where they encountered departed relatives in the mirror.

"HE MOVED RIGHT OUT OF THE MIRROR"

An example of both these phenomena, that of encountering an unexpected person and that of an apparition coming out of the mirror, comes from a businessman who described himself as an "interested skeptic." He had come to the Theater of the Mind to attempt a visionary reunion with his father, who had died when this subject was only twelve years old. He had admired his father greatly and said that only in the past twenty years had he been able to cope with the feelings of abandonment that arose after his death.

We spent a long day preparing for the reunion, sorting through family photographs and looking at pictures of furniture his father had made. There were fond remembrances of childhood visits to the park and drives to a grandmother's house in the country. That evening he went into the apparition booth. When he came out, he had an amazing story to tell:

> I sat in the booth a little while before I got the hang of it. It's like you told me, if you try to make it happen or sit there thinking about whether it's going to happen, it won't. It was just about the time I was going to get up and come back in here that I thought, "I'll stay a little while longer," and I settled in. I believe it was that settling in that started it, but just about the time I wasn't worried about it happening anymore was when it started up.

I saw this mist in there, and to tell you the truth, for just a minute I thought you were going to have to call the fire department because it looked like smoke to me. I finally saw it was in the mirror, but for just an instant I thought it was smoke. Then I saw colors all over the mirror, patches of color, and I began to see scenes. Some were of my childhood. They were very realistic. Three-dimensional scenes were all around me. Some of them I recognized as things in my life, but others not.

One was of my father a long time ago, sitting on the porch steps. I remembered that happening, so this was just a memory but a clear memory, right out in front of me. I could almost touch it. I felt like I could anyway. But I didn't feel he was there; this was just a memory in the mirror.

There were scenes, too, of places I have never been to or seen. Very pretty places. I don't know where they were or what this was, but I got to thinking that the scenes were all around me on the sides, so I was in the mirror.

At the place I went into the mirror, I felt refreshed, as if I were a new me. I knew someone was there with me, but I had no idea who. Then I saw this shape, a person forming I could see him a little bit at a time. It seemed he was moving into the light.

Now this is going to sound strange, but I thought I was the one in the mirror and he was the one coming out of the apparition room.

Very definitely the man who was coming into

focus was in the apparition room. For a moment I thought I was in the mirror, but then I came back into the apparition room, too, and this man just about my size was in there with me. This was a continuous movement for him. He moved into the light and right out of the mirror into the apparition room in a smooth motion. He popped right out. I was the one who was moving back and forth in and out of the mirror for just a minute until I settled back into the room and was sitting in my chair again.

I must have jumped because when I could see who it was, it was my old business partner. He was about two years younger than I was, and we had worked together for fifteen years. Then one day his wife went home and found him in the shower dead of a heart attack.

He had been a young man of thirty-eight, and they had four children.

It is funny, but while we were working together, I didn't think of him as a good friend. We were just business partners. But when he died, I went down into the dumps. My wife later told me that they were afraid they were going to have to put me in the hospital for a while.

Anyway, when he came into the apparition booth, I saw him clearly. He was about two feet away from me. I was so surprised I couldn't think what to do. It was him, right there. He was my size, and I saw him from the waist up. He had a full form and he was not transparent. He moved around, and when he did, I could see his head and arms move, all in three dimensions.

He looked just as he had when he died, but maybe a little younger. There was an appearance as if all blemishes had been removed, and he was very lively.

He was happy to see me. I was amazed, but he didn't seem amazed. He knew what was going on, was my impression. He wanted to reassure me. He was telling me not to worry, that he was fine. I know that his thought was that we would be together again. His wife is dead now, too, and he was sending me the thought that she was with him, but for some reason I was not supposed to see her.

I didn't hear any words or noises. This was all in thoughts that were passed back and forth, but there wasn't any point in using words.

I asked him several questions. I wanted to know something about his daughter that had always concerned me. I had kept in touch with three of the children and helped them out. But there was some difficulty with his second daughter. I had reached out to her, but she blamed me some for her father's death. As she grew older, she said we had worked too hard. So I asked him what to do, and he gave me complete reassurance about what I wanted to know, and it cleared some things up for me.

When it was over, he vanished quickly, and I was up out of that chair. I was shaking a little bit when I came out because I was excited. I felt that was him.

It was exactly like him being there, as far as I am concerned.

I didn't have any sense of my father being in there, but my partner sure was. I couldn't think what to do or how to behave. But I do feel that I have made my peace with my partner.

This man insisted that the apparition in the booth was no apparition at all but was actually his business partner. He based this feeling on the answers he received to some of his questions. These were answers he had searched for on his own for years. Finally, after a few moments with the apparition of his business partner, he had the answers he had been looking for.

"I still want to see my father," he said. "But apparently my need to see my old business partner was greater than I thought."

About six months later this man told me that his experience in the psychomanteum continued to have a powerful impact on him. He repeated his statement that it had enabled him to "make my peace" with his partner and said that he had "put to rest" his worries about the partner's family.

He still often thought about his visit to the psycho-manteum, he said, and was completely confident that he had really been in the presence of his friend that day.

Actual conversations took place Never once during my research did it enter my mind that the subjects might communicate with the presences they visited at the psychomanteum. Yet in almost 50 percent of the cases, complex communications were reported. These ranged from a few words of reassurance and love to lengthy and involved communications, even to conversational exchanges.

In approximately 15 percent of the cases the subjects said that they actually heard the voice of the deceased person. I don't mean that they heard it in the way that one hears one's own thoughts. I mean they heard it as though it were audible. Others report the communication as a sort of telepathy, as though the apparitions and the subjects immediately understood each other's thoughts and feelings without needing to speak.

Apparitions appear later   Roughly 25 percent of those seeking reunions don't have them until after they have left the psychomanteum. This means that they see the departed loved one when they have returned to their hotel room or home, or, in my case, when I went into another room. Usually such a reunion takes place within twenty-four hours.

"I REALIZED I WAS HAVING AN APPARITION"

For example, a well-respected journalist in her early sixties came to the Theater of the Mind in hopes of seeing her son, who had committed suicide about a year earlier.

As you will see from her remarkable story, nothing happened for several hours, until she left the psychomanteum:

I had the apparition of my son several hours after I had been in the apparition booth, and to this day I can see it as clearly as I can see the coffeepot I am looking at right now. I can see that face. If I were an artist, I could draw it.

When I got back to the hotel where I was staying, I made a few phone calls because I was very excited about the day I had spent at the Theater of the Mind, and I wanted to call home. Then I went to bed and fell sound asleep.

I don't know exactly what time it was that I woke up, but when I did, I felt a presence in the room, and there was this young man standing in the room, between the television set and the dresser.

At first he was pretty expressionless, and he was looking at me. I was so frightened my heart was going a hundred miles a minute. I am glad I was in a king-size bed because I think I would have fallen off the bed, I was so scared.

What was going through my mind was, "Oh, God, there must be another entrance to the room!" That's how real he was, standing there.

This was no dream. I was wide awake. I saw him clearly, his whole body, except I didn't see his feet. I looked at him and he looked at me. I don't know how long it was, but it was long enough for me to be frightened, and I don't frighten easily.

But then I realized that I was having an apparition, that this was my son. It didn't look like him at first, but putting everything together, I realized it was him. As a matter of fact, it looked exactly like him as he had looked about ten years earlier.

It became very peaceful after that. I was very assured about my son, that he is okay and that he loves me. This was a turning point for me. It was a wonderful experience.

Reunions are thought of as "real"   To my amazement it became clear that the visionary reunions were being experienced as real events, not fantasies or dreams. So far almost all of the subjects have asserted that their encounters were completely real and that they had actually been in the living presence of loved ones lost to death.

The person who has undergone this experience is powerfully affected by it   Although the subject is guided through this experience in a clinical setting, I think he or she is having a spiritual experience of a positive and transformative nature. All the indications are there:

- A paranormal event has taken place that shakes the foundation of the subject's reality.
- It is a positive experience that has spoken to a deep spiritual need.
- It changes the subject's outlook on the meaning of life.

My observations and intuitions tell me that the changes that take place in a person who mirror-gazes are similar to those that take place in a person who has had a near-death experience. Such people become kinder, more understanding, and less afraid of death.

"I FELT SO HAPPY, I WANTED TO SHOUT"

The "realness" of an experience and the depths to which it can affect emotions is illustrated by a woman of twenty-six, who came to seek a reunion with her favorite aunt, Betty. Along with others in the family, she had worried that this aunt, who had died alone, might have suffered and been unable to summon help during her last hours. She, too, traveled into the mirror during her visionary reunion.

I felt nervous in there [the apparition room] initially, but I calmed down pretty quickly. I didn't really expect it would work in my case. That kind of thing is always something that happens to someone else you know. But you know, it really did start happening right away. The visions, if that's what they were, seemed plain as day. There was nothing unreal about this, but it sure is hard to explain.

I saw visions first in the mirror, well, at first color patterns and little bright flickers or specks flashing. I saw this big mist just come in and fill up the whole mirror, just like a big fog blowing right up over the window, and after the mist was a bright light. I saw a light in the far distance and scenery, little brief scenes, but then my attention was drawn to a pathway, and I knew I was to go down that way or off in that direction.

I moved on that way. I can't say I went into the mirror because I didn't notice going through it, but I know for sure I was in this other dimension. The light and other scenes were all around, but I didn't pay them any attention because I knew I had to get down that passageway.

I moved on through, and I saw these three people standing off a little to my left side, and I moved up closer to them, and there I saw that it was my grandmother and my favorite aunt, Betty, who died, and this other person I didn't recognize, but a woman definitely.

Aunt Betty kind of indicated to me that this person was my great-grandmother Harriet and then I knew because I had seen her photographs. She didn't really look just like the pictures, though. She was more active-looking than in the pictures I saw or what I imagined. She looked real young, but she had been very old when she died. I had always heard the family talking about her since I was a little girl. This woman was a real strong presence.

I felt so happy, just like I wanted to shout out. It was great to see Betty and my grandmother. They both seemed to understand so much, if you know what I mean. A lot more knowledgeable than when they were alive.

I was so overjoyed during this whole meeting. I was so happy. There was not a doubt in the world they were there and that I saw them, and it was as real as meeting anyone. I couldn't reach to touch them from where I was.

They told me everything was okay and they were fine. That was a real relief for me. I can say now I am not worried about her. She was really relaxed and calm.

If I could only describe that light to you. I've never seen anything like that. I didn't get all the way into the light. I saw all this from a little distance. I didn't hear any voices, I just knew what they were trying to tell me. It was more like what I have heard of as thought reading.

I had a little time with my grandmother too. I was one of her first grandchildren, so we had a special bond. She was saying, too, that she is fine. It was just a happy reunion.

They all looked like regular people. I saw them clearly, up close but not right up on them. I knew that I was not with them to stay, but I realized then that they were still alive and I would see them again. I didn't see their feet, just from the knees up.

This didn't last a very long time. Then I just came back into the chair, and the visions in the mirror faded away quickly. You sure have given me a lot to think about. I never would have believed such a thing. There isn't any question it was real, though.

112

They were right there in front of me, and it was them.

Fourteen months after her visit this woman told me that she'd had two other brief encounters with apparitions of her aunt Betty. Neither was as elaborate as the one she had had at the psychomanteum, but in both cases she felt the presence of her aunt. Her visit to the psychomanteum and its aftermath have changed her mind about the paranormal. Where before she had doubts about an aferlife, she is now persuaded of a life beyond death.

Do these transformations last long? I don't know, since I will have to observe the people who have mirror-gazed for several years to answer that question. I can say for now that successful apparitional facilitation leads at least to a short-term transformation in personality.

VARIETIES OF EXPERIENCE

The analyses I have provided of the various phenomena and percentages of facilitated visionary reunions were only developed gradually as visitors came one after the other to the psychomanteum. To me it is remembered as a continuous flow of memorable time spent with sensitive and accomplished people.

It has been fascinating to watch reasonable people relate fresh, firsthand accounts of what had seemed to them to be real events of a highly unusual nature. As I review them, they are unforgettable tales.

"THEY WERE WAITING FOR SOMEONE"

One of my earliest subjects was a man in his early seventies whose career in psychotherapy had been long and distinguished. I mention this to point out that he had an acute and seasoned understanding of the human mind.

We prepared all day in hopes that he might visit that evening with his father who had died three decades before. Together we looked at faded photographs and perused old documents. We discussed his fond, and not-so-fond memories of his father. Around dusk I escorted him into the apparition chamber. When he emerged about an hour and a half later, he was visibly moved, yet quite happy about his astounding voyage into the Middle Realm.

I was in there some while before anything started, how long I don't know. After a while it seemed that the mirror was clouding up with mist, like swirls of fine dust. And that just vanished and I saw forms like geometrical designs floating around moment-arily. I felt a kind of jerk or shudder, vertigo, like maybe I was going to get dizzy, but I didn't.

I moved forward, not with a lurch but smoothly, almost gliding. I moved right on through.

Pretty soon I caught sight of something way ahead through the darkness. Well, none of this was com-pletely dark. Everything was lit up but off in the distance this one spot was brightest, so the other

114

looked darker by comparison. I was moving on through this not-so-bright place toward that light, and as I got closer and closer, I began to see it was almost a structure of some kind. I can't tell you what it was. I plainly saw it, but I can't put it into words for you.

It was something like a platform or a stage. I thought of the platform at the train station where people were waiting for someone to come in on the train, all lit up in this soft, bright or yellowish white light.

I was still moving toward this platform trying to see what it was and wondering what in hell was going on, but then I saw these two people on the platform, looking off into the distance like they were waiting for someone. Then, as I got closer, I recognized them as my cousins I had been so close to, Harry and Ruth.

All of a sudden I was walking, or I felt that I was walking, out onto this platform, and as I did so, they lit up and came toward me, but only so far. I don't know how to say this, but the whole time there was some kind of barricade or shield perhaps between them and me. I didn't see anything, but I sensed an obstruction there! I got the idea I wasn't supposed to go over it or through it, nor were they either.

They both recognized me right away. It seemed they were waiting for someone when I first saw them, and it seemed they were expecting me. They didn't say hello, but there sure was a greeting. They knew full well I was there.

I felt so joyful. They looked a lot younger than when they died, more as they had in our younger years when we were all good friends. Still, there was a difference. They looked a little different, healthier you might say, or as though they had a lot of energy, a lot of life.

I understood that they meant to say they were fine and glad to see me and that we would be together again someday. I didn't hear any words, though. These were all thought communications.

I felt happy, and I knew they did too. Then suddenly I was drawn backward, and I saw them receding off into the distance again and I felt myself sitting in the chair again.

When I asked him how the encounter felt, he said it was in no way like a dream. It seemed so real to him that he was convinced that he had been in the presence of his cousins. He remarked at least twice that when he first glimpsed them, they seemed to be waiting for him.

This story has a sad footnote. A few months later a friend of this man contacted me to say that he had been killed in an automobile accident. As I assembled his case study for this book, I couldn't help wondering if the vision of his cousins waiting expectantly for him had somehow presaged his death.

"I WAS SEEING HIM RIGHT UP ON ME"

A woman in her late forties who wanted to see her deceased father reported an encounter that is typical of out-of-mirror experiences, in which a figure seems to emerge from the mirror and enter the apparition booth:

When I went in there, I was a little bit scared. Why I don't know, because I have been anticipating this day for over a month now, and maybe it was the feeling that the time had finally come.

When we were in the study going through my father's mementos, I felt a kind of certainty come over me, and even then I knew that I would see him. It was like I knew all along that he would be there. When I was showing you the jewelry box he made for my birthday, I felt it would be a sure thing.

But going into the apparition booth made me a little bit scared. After all, this is a strange thing for me to be doing. The people at the office where I work would never believe I'd be doing something like this. I hardly believe it myself, except that I had so many loose ends to tie up with Dad that he has been pretty much constantly on my mind since he died.

Once I got into the room, I don't think it was long at all before I started seeing things. There were colors mostly at first and pretty clouds, and then once in a while I would catch a glimpse of a passing scene.

I remember seeing a little village that looked like it would be in England or maybe France, but old, this place was very old. I had the feeling I was peering back into time.

The people walking around were dressed up in

old-time clothing. I would guess medieval or before. I saw one man walk right by me, right in front of my eyes, and he was shooing a bunch of cows along with a worried look on his face. I don't have any idea where all that was coming from. I'm not a farm girl.

All those little scenes hurried past, but when my dad came up in the mirror, that was different. He was not fleeting like the others. He just came up suddenly, and I was looking right into his face.

He talked to me, and he was funny like he always was. He asked me, "Why in the world are you trying to talk to me, girl?"

I can't say I heard a voice like I'm hearing you talk, but it was stronger than thoughts. I can't say that we needed words. I just could tell what he was trying to say.

He was always testy, but it was in a funny way. He was always making jokes or having something funny to say. So this was just like him.

He had a big smile on his face when I saw him. As funny as it sounds to say it, he was right there in that room with me, I know he was.

He looked to be about three feet away, but then he got closer. I wasn't seeing him in the mirror; I was seeing him right up on me.

We had some very personal conversations in there about my mother mainly, but other family matters as well. It seemed like the most natural thing in the world, just like the conversations we used to have in the parlor when I was a teenager or even after I got married. Except now he is dead!

I just saw his head and chest and upper abdomen area. It was not his whole form, but this was just as clear as looking at you. I still felt there was something between us, an energy or something like that. I say that because I was afraid that if I reached out to touch him, he wouldn't stay.

I just sat there a long time carrying on back and forth with him. He seemed a little bit amused, like he thought I was being impatient by wanting to talk to him now rather than waiting until I died and passed over. That was a switch, because always before I was the patient one and he wanted things to happen right then and to hurry along. When I think about it, maybe he was teasing me for being impatient the way I had teased him.

I talked to him a long time, maybe thirty minutes. But it went so fast.

The last thing he said to me was, "Now you go on and enjoy your life." I felt so good when he said that. There was a flood of relief and good feelings that came rushing in. I don't believe I've felt so good since he died. It was as though something just closed off, and the pain of his death was over. Then he disappeared and there was just the mirror.

In some respects this woman's encounter closely parallels another facilitated apparition described by a woman in her mid-fifties. Notice the similarities:

"MY MOM CAME OUT OF THE MIRROR"

I saw a vision of my mother years ago, before I even tried mirror gazing. She committed suicide in 1975. My grandfather, her father, had been a minister, so I was raised with the idea that suicide was the most unforgivable sin. So when she passed away, I was upset that I had lost her but was more upset that she was lost forever.

When I walked into the service at the funeral home, I was really in such a state of grief over that. But a little voice—I call it a little voice from God—spoke to me and I looked up to my right, and way up toward the ceiling was a vision of my mother and Christ, walking hand in hand away from me. It was in full color and just as natural as life. They both looked over their shoulders, and then they smiled at me and disappeared.

That is what started my spiritual quest. At that particular moment I knew that many things I had been told were not true.

Not quite a year later my husband, Bill, was killed. We had been married ten years. This was definitely my dark night of the soul. Since that time I have been on a spiritual path.

I have meditated for long periods of time and have tried to go to a deep level of meditation to communicate with my husband, so I was calm about going into the apparition booth.

I don't know how long I was in there before

something happened, maybe ten or fifteen minutes, maybe not that long. But after a while I lost sight of the mirror, and instead I saw my mom.

First I saw her from a long distance away, and it was just her face. Then, as she came closer and closer, she was more ghostly, but not in a haunting way. She was not as bright and not as solid. Plus there was a kind of smokiness around her.

She smiled and called me Birdie, which is what she called me when I was young. "Birdie," she said, "I have come to see you because Bill is not able to come. I am a little farther along than he is, and he still has a lot to learn. He is studying. But he's all right and he loves you very much and he's fine."

At that particular point she just kind of came out of the mirror. It was as if she was just right there. She had a wonderful look on her face. She was radiant.

I became extremely warm, and I didn't know if that was because I was so excited or if it was the energy around her. The voice was different from you and me talking. The best I can describe it is that I worked for years as an overseas operator for the telephone company. When we bounced signals off the satellite, it had a different quality of sound to it. That is how this was.

What happened was not imagination. It was as real as real and very reverent.

The funny thing is that my mom was close enough that I could have touched her. I don't know what would have happened had I tried. I was just so spellbound and was really concentrating on what she had to say and making eye contact that I didn't think to reach out. I wish that I had now to see what would have happened.

I don't think I talked to her out loud. I think I just said things in my mind, but I cannot really be sure. She answered me so quickly that I don't think I had time to speak. Mostly it seemed like a one-way conversation, her to me. It was as if I was in a limbo of sorts, just mostly in awe and studying everything that was going on.

My time in the booth lasted maybe thirty or forty minutes. When it came to an end, the whole scene turned to a fine mist and she disappeared.

This experience changed this woman's life for the better. She has become more relaxed and pleasant to be around. In times of stress she is able to see her mother again when she meditates. "I usually see Mom during times of difficult problems. She comforts me by saying 'It's okay,' or 'You'll be all right.' It's good to have her around."

"ALL OF THEM LOOKED VERY MUCH ALIVE"

A young man, twenty-six years old, who was surrounded by apparitions of deceased relatives, did try to touch them. He had come to the psychomanteum in hopes of seeing a sister who had died. Here is his story in his own words:

I was sitting in there, and all of a sudden it seemed that these three people stepped right into the room all around me. It looked as if they stepped out of the mirror but I felt that such a thing couldn't be, so I was shocked. I didn't know what was going on.

For a moment I thought it was you trying to play a joke on me. So I reached up quickly, trying to touch them and when I did, my hand hit the curtain.

I still saw them. I got a look at all three. My sister, Jill, was there, but two others also, my friend Todd and my grandfather. All of them looked very much alive, just looking at me.

I didn't hear any voices or really communicate with them. It happened so fast, and I was so shocked. They didn't say anything, but they all looked so good, and I felt they were trying to get across to me that they were fine.

The light around them was different, not like regular light. They were lit up. They seemed very happy. This was completely real. I felt their presence too. It was just like they were there in the room with me.

This man might well have empathized with Odysseus' frustration at trying to embrace his mother. He has since begun to wonder what the experience would have been like had he not tried to touch the apparitions. He now plans to repeat the experience, this time letting the vision run its course.

TAKE-OUT VISIONS

A forty-four-year-old woman came to the psycho-manteum to see her husband, who had died two years earlier. We prepared all day long by discussing their relationship. That evening she went into the apparition booth. An hour later she emerged with the disappointing story of having seen some faint visions of what she thought was a man. There was no communication, and the image disappeared quickly.

It wasn't what happened in the booth that is interesting with this subject, however. Like some of the others, she had a "take-out" vision, an apparition that appeared to her at a later date.

Here is her story:

When I was in there, I kept thinking that I saw something off to my right in the mirror. When I looked at the mirror and tried to focus, the image disappeared. Then I started gazing again, and I saw something that looked like it was at my right shoulder. When I turned to look, it was gone. It did look like a person, but I couldn't tell who it was.

Then I saw another image. I knew it was a man, but I had no feeling whatsoever as to who it was. In fact at first I thought it was you coming in to check on me.

This man was both in and out of the mirror. He emerged, and that's why I turned and looked to my right. This was not like a reflection. It was a real form coming out of the mirror, but when I turned to look again, it was gone.

At that point I gave up. I came downstairs and was real disappointed because I thought it didn't work.

Then I went home. That first night I started having the distinct feeling that someone was around. I would go to sleep, and it was as though I felt someone in the room. I would wake up still feeling that someone had been in there with me, but I couldn't figure out who it was.

On the second night I woke up and had a strong sense of the presence of my father in the room. I could tell that he was trying to talk to me, but I couldn't tell what he was saying. After waking up that time I couldn't go back to sleep.

The next night it happened again. This was the third night in a row in which I went to sleep and woke up feeling a presence in the room. This time I woke up and smelled my father's aftershave lotion.

I was completely awake, and this was not a dream, it was very concrete, very here and now.

I looked up, and my father was standing at the door of my bedroom. I had been lying on the bed but I stood up and walked over to him. I was within four steps of him. He looked just like my dad, but not sickly like he had been just before he died. He was full figure, but he looked more fleshed out than when he died. He looked whole, like everything was wonderful.

125

I didn't hear his voice, but I understood what he was saying. He didn't want me to worry. I got the distinct impression that he was telling me that everything was okay.

I had been very bothered because my dad had died by himself. There was nobody there, and there were a lot of problems at the time of his death, like questions about whether he'd had enough oxygen to make it through the night. That bothered me badly because I am the only child and my mom and dad were separated.

But seeing him that night, I really got the distinct impression that he was okay and that he was telling me that I shouldn't worry about him, that everything was fine. I just knew his thoughts and he knew mine.

And then he just went away. I was awake for quite a while after that. I felt as though I had really been in his presence, and I didn't want to lose that.

This woman was somewhat perplexed by the experience. She had prepared to see her late husband and saw an apparition of her father instead. She now realizes that maybe mirror gazing won't allow her to be so selective.

"It was as if I had a big pie pan in front of my face and I had poked a little hole in it and said, 'I want to see my husband,'" she said. "Instead I had to leave it open to whoever would come to me."

Since her mirror-gazing experience this woman has felt

very peaceful about her father. She no longer feels guilt and anxiety when thinking about him. "Now I have a neat feeling when I think about him," she said, "a real connection."

This type of experience, which is reminiscent of dream incubation, has turned out to be a recurring pattern among visitors to the psychomanteum.

It typically happens to someone who has little or nothing happen in the apparition booth; that is, there occurs a dramatic visitation upon returning home.

"THERE WAS JANE NEXT TO THE BED"

Another take-out vision occurred to a man in his late fifties who had lost his daughter five years before under very tragic circumstances. He came to my facility because he had been unable to resolve his grief after her death.

He did not see her while in the apparition booth. Two days later, however, I received a telephone call from him describing a fascinating encounter that had happened the previous evening.

I went to bed about eleven-thirty, right after the late news on television, and I fell asleep almost as soon as my head hit the pillow. The next thing I knew, I woke up and sat bolt upright in bed. I knew that my daughter was in the room. I looked at the clock and noticed that it was two thirty-seven A.M.

There was Jane right there next to the bed. I had the feeling I used to have when she would come home from college and would arrive home late and come into our room. It was like she was coming home from college and just dropped in to say hello.

She looked wonderful. She was shining, just lit up beautifully. She was happy and sparkling. She kept telling me, "You've got to calm down. Calm down just a minute."

I didn't hear her voice, not even a sound. But she was directing these thoughts at me, and the thoughts were so strong that it was almost like having them.

The light from the street was coming through the blinds, and I could see her well. Now, I've got to tell you that I was completely awake the whole time, there is no question. And you know I am not one for imagining things.

This was my daughter. She was telling me that all was well, that she is fine. I got the idea, or she was saying, that death isn't at all like I thought it was. She was happy and smiling. She kept telling me, "Be calm. I can't be here long, but there's nothing to worry about. I'm fine."

And that was it. She said, "Good-bye for now," and she was gone.

The experience lasted four minutes by the clock, and when the girl disappeared, she did so instantaneously, "like a switch being turned off."

The man is convinced that what happened was no

apparition but was really his daughter. As a result much of his sadness about her sudden loss has been soothed. "This wasn't a dream, it was an experience like you would have with any human being," he said. "I have no doubt that I will see her again someday."

APPARITIONS IN MANY FORMS

Because of experiences like these, I have adopted the policy of informing visitors to the psychomanteum that it is possible that they will experience apparitions after they return home.

In fact with every new visitor to the Theater of the Mind, I am learning more about evoking apparitions of the deceased, and I continue to revise the procedure accordingly.

I also explain to apparition seekers that spontaneous apparitions come in many forms and can grace all of the senses too. Most of these are visual, in which a person actually *sees* an apparition of the departed. A high percentage of apparitions are auditory (27 percent, according to one study), followed in frequency by those that are tactile (13 percent).

The next three cases are examples of auditory experiences.

"HE'S TOO EMBARRASSED TO TALK"

A psychiatrist in her late thirties came to the psycho-manteum in hopes of seeing her father, who in his last years had been verbally abusive and accusatory toward members of his family.

As a way of inspiring memory the psychiatrist brought an example of her father's woodworking and some family photos. The father had died three years before, and for some years prior to that the relationship between the two of them had been very tense and conflicted. In light of this bad relationship the results of her gazing session were intriguing:

> I sat in there for quite a while before anything happened. I saw various images and forms and colors in the mirror, patterns mostly. Then, after a while, I was surprised to hear my grandmother suddenly start talking to me. I distinctly heard her voice, which I haven't heard for years since she died.
>
> I said, "Grandmother, is that you?"
>
> And she said, "Yes, it is." Then she said, "I'm here with Howard and Kathleen [my late aunt and uncle], and your father is here too."
>
> I said, "Can he come to talk to me?"
>
> "No," she said, "he's too embarrassed to talk."
>
> I feel sure that my father was embarrassed because of his cold-shouldering attitude to his children the last eight years of his life. I think he also had some paranoid ideas about his loved ones that were not true. He believed on some level that we were out to get him.
>
> It is obvious to me from the conversation I had with my grandmother that he knows we weren't that

way and is probably embarrassed at how he was and some of the things he said, which were terrible.

About the experience itself: I've heard a lot of schizophrenic patients talking about voices, but so often they are talking about commanding voices or critical voices or just mumbles and buzzes.

My grandmother's voice wasn't like any of those. It sounded exactly like her voice. It was like she was near. It was strange, though. I wasn't expecting her at all, yet I had the feeling of her being right in the booth with me.

"IT WAS EXACTLY LIKE SHE WAS THERE"

Another visitor to my oracle of the dead who heard a preternatural voice was a man in his mid-twenties, who came to see a girlfriend who had been killed when the two were teenagers. Although he did not see the girl, his experience was satisfying anyway.

After what I guess was no more than five minutes I began to hear the voice of this friend of mine who was killed in a boating accident. It was just like her speaking to me. I'm not talking here about thoughts or daydreams or imagination. I've never heard anything like it.

She just talked to me and said it was wonderful where she was. I could hear each word plainly and separately. There was a quality to it, like an echo, I believe, like maybe she was speaking through a tin tube. It was her voice, though, definitely.

I had felt very bad about her death. All of our friends had. Nobody among my friends or family had died before, so this was the first time something like this had ever happened to me. I wished I had been able to say good-bye or told her that I cared.

So this was a wonderful experience. There was a complete reassurance, just like being with her. I didn't see her, but it was exactly like she was there.

"IT WAS DIRECT EMOTIONAL CONTACT"

I was particularly excited about performing a facilitated apparition with this next subject, since she was the first person I worked with who'd had a near-death experience. Her story was a sad one. Just a few months after her younger sister was killed in an automobile accident, this subject was also nearly killed in an auto accident. She'd had a near-death experience as a result of that accident and saw her late sister. This contact came after she left her body and resulted in a deep emotional experience of the type she had never known before. As she described it, "I found that the physical body actually keeps emotions from getting in. When I was out of my body, my emotions were raw. When I was out of my body, it was as if my emotions were meeting her emotions. It was direct emotional contact."

I was intrigued by the opportunity to facilitate an apparition with this subject because it would allow me to compare the results of mirror gazing with a near-death experience. Here is her apparitional facilitation as she described it:

> I felt the mirror rising at first. It kept going up. Then I saw images coming out in the form of shapes and flashes of light. Then I saw a red light with a green mist in the center. And then I heard my little sister say, "I am here."
>
> I said in my mind, "I would like to see you." And she said, "Well, I am here."
>
> So I tried to relax, but I could never physically see her. But I felt her! I felt her kiss me on the cheek the way we always did when she was alive. And then I heard her say, "I am here."
>
> I couldn't see her, but I knew she was there. I could feel the love of her presence. I had a little flashback too. I saw us sitting in her room listening to records. I also saw us practicing cheers that helped her get on the cheerleading team. I felt love at this point, the same kind of love I felt when the actual events were going on.

I asked this subject to compare the mirror vision with her near-death experience. In the NDE she had seen her sister, whereas in the apparition booth she had only heard and felt her. But on an emotional level there was little difference, she said. "It was like hearing a physical voice.

I could hear her speaking. It was as if she was leaning in and talking in my ear."

FOR GRIEF AND KNOWLEDGE

The word *psychomanteum*, taken literally, implies that the spirits of the dead are summoned as a means of divination so that they can be asked questions about the future or other hidden knowledge. Purists will quibble that the facility I created for this study is not a psychomanteum since our purpose was not to arouse the dead for divination. Rather people came (and still come) in hopes of satisfying a longing for the company of those whom they have lost to death. Whatever the difference in intention between those ancient institutions and the contemporary one that I have built, I suspect that they converge insofar as their day-to-day operation is concerned.

Through my work with facilitated apparitions I have come to realize the important place grief can occupy in human life. The Greek historian Plutarch tells a touching story that illustrates this very point. A prominent and wealthy man, Elysius, was obsessed with the thought that perhaps his young son, who had died, had been murdered with poison. In his torment Elysius went to what is now southern Italy to a psychomanteum that apparently employed a form of dream incubation. After conducting the prescribed rituals, Elysius fell asleep and had a vision. His father appeared to him, coming toward him. Elysius told his father everything that had happened and begged him to find out the cause of the boy's death. Elysius's father was followed by a young man. Just as has happened on several occasions in my psychomanteum, Elysius at first did not recognize this person, who turned out to be his son. The young man's identity became obvious, and he assured his father that his death had been from natural causes.

I believe that our reasons for being interested in visionary reunions are no different from those of the ancient Greeks. I am sure that, then as now, most sought not knowledge but adventure, consolation, completion, and even solace in the psychomanteum.

FIVE

A ROAD TO SELF-DISCOVERY

I seemed to walk among a world of ghosts,
And feel myself the shadow of a dream.
—Alexis Tolstoy

In our modern world, reflection and meditation have taken a backseat to technology. The hectic pace of life has caused us to lose touch with ourselves in a very real way. The struggle just to keep up has led people to have difficulty making contact with their inner feelings. This is where mirror gazing can help. Mirror visions that result from a sort of free-form gazing (not visionary facilitation) sometimes lead to insights into that deep inner well known as the unconscious mind.

"I SENSED AN EXTREME FEAR"

A forty-four-year-old woman whom I introduced to mirror gazing started experimenting with the procedure on her own. She had been looking for the key to her own psychological dilemma for years through traditional psychotherapy. After several sessions of mirror gazing she recovered a memory that led to great advances in self-understanding. Here is her story:

> When I tried mirror gazing, I found that intense feelings would come up. It became clear that I was tuning in to some feelings that I had blocked out during ordinary consciousness.
>
> I sensed an extreme fear, but I wasn't sure what the fear was. At times I would literally jump up and leave because I was afraid of what it was I was going to see.
>
> Specifically I found that it was a fear of having to go on by myself and take care of myself. I also had a horrible fear of failure.
>
> What I saw were different faces and different situations. Each one showed how eaten up by fear I was.
>
> During one session I saw a pattern with the way I related to people. This started in my childhood and had to do with being the oldest child and having to take care of the other children in the family.
>
> I saw myself before my brothers were born, being the apple of everyone's eye. Then my brothers came along, and all of that switched. People began paying attention to them and not to me. To get my father's attention and approval, I became the caregiver. In one image I could see myself giving them baths while my parents sat in the living room.

As a way of being accommodating I always placed myself second in my relationship with males. Whenever the relationship needed to be saved, I was the one who made the effort. I could see times during which I did things that I didn't want to do just to please the men in my life.

Then I saw an event that was coming up in my family. My great-aunt is about to be ninety, and my mother and brother are planning a weekend party for her. In the speculum I saw myself jumping in and taking charge. I saw myself calling my mom and telling her that I would bring the dinner for Friday night.

These images caused me pain. I realized that in my relationships, my so-called friends and relatives didn't come to me to have fun, they came to get me to help them with something. Through mirror gazing I realized that I had become weighed down with burdens, that I wasn't having any fun.

This woman changed many patterns in her life after her visionary experience. She stopped volunteering for duties that she didn't find pleasurable. Instead of jumping in and taking charge at family get-togethers, she enjoyed herself and let others run the show. The same was true of her relationship with her children, for whom she had made so many decisions. Now she let them make their own mistakes with little input from her. "Now instead of telling them what to do, I just make suggestions and drop it," she said.

SYMBOL VISIONS

The experience just described was in "real," not symbolic, images. This makes it easier for the person having them, since there is little to interpret. Symbolic visions that emerge during mirror gazing are more difficult to clarify. Once it is done, they can be just as rewarding as visions with no symbolic content. Sometimes they can even be more rewarding than "real" visions, since they allow a person freedom to talk about a wide variety of things in his or her life that can relate to these symbols.

As you can see, the following mirror vision is full of symbolic content:

> I am deeply afraid of snakes. Several times during my gazing a snake would form.
>
> During one of my visions the house I was raised in was being attacked by a snake that was almost as big as a house. It was rising up and hissing and throwing its tongue out as if it were going to bite. Then coming along next to it was another that was just as big. It was different from the other one. It was blue and had beautiful blue eyes, and it was smiling.
>
> As I looked, I thought, "Isn't that sweet?" But then I felt the fear and I ran. I didn't trust it.

We discussed the vision when it was over. With surprisingly little hesitation the woman said that the images in the mirror had to do with trust.

"It is almost like I am afraid that people are going to

appear one way and then turn against me," she said, referring to the different personalities of the two snakes. "I don't trust people. I think they are going to be one way and they become another. I feel deceived."

"I SAW A PEACOCK!"

Another symbolic mirror vision came from a woman who was interested in mirror gazing just to "see what will come out." I was glad to help her, since I am intrigued by the visions people have when they are not searching for anything in particular. When this is done, it provides an excellent opportunity to assess the results of mirror gazing on normal people who are simply interested in self-exploration.

This woman was a twenty-three-year-old graduate of a southern university. She claimed to have no strong religious background and no particular interest in the subject. My guess, however, is that she was searching for some kind of spirituality. I base my opinion on the content of her mirror vision. Here it is:

> I sat down [in the gazing booth] and did some deep breathing and relaxing, maybe for about five minutes. Then all I could see was the frame of the mirror and the blackness in the mirror itself. I stared at it for some time, and then these shadows began dancing around. Then the shadows came out of the mirror and danced in the booth with me!
>
> Soon the vision in the mirror got gray and misty.

Then the mirror started moving in segments. Parts of it started going away from me while parts came toward me. Then I couldn't see the frame of the mirror anymore, and I realized that the mirror had just engulfed me. I was inside the mirror!

Then I saw a peacock. It was facing away from me. Then it turned around, and I was overwhelmed by the colors. It turned and spread its feathers out. It was huge!

It seemed to have a human face, although I couldn't see exactly what the face looked like. Then I saw something else behind the peacock. I could see what looked like a black person up on a sacrificial altar. The person was lying with his arms and head hanging off the sides of this altar and he appeared to be dead. His face was turned toward me, but it was covered with hair, so I couldn't see the features.

Then the mirror came toward me again. All I saw was a big triangle like a dinner bell and a little metal piece like the one used to ring the bell. Then the bell rang for what seemed like a couple of minutes. It rang slowly, like a church bell, and was so relaxing that I almost fell asleep.

Before that happened, though, I found myself dancing with Jesus Christ! And when I looked around, I was dancing with him at the Last Supper! We danced around the table, and then a black woman came and led me away.

As with many subjects this one found gazing to be one of the most relaxing experiences she had ever had. And although she said that she didn't understand the meaning of the visions, I think she was just trying to come to grips with the role of religion in her life, the peacock, for example, is an ancient symbol of Christ. And her description of it being "huge" and overwhelmingly beautiful is a pleasant one and implies to me that she is drawn to the caring message of Christianity that lies beneath much of the doctrine that she has always rejected. In addition, the fact that her image of Christ was of a religious figure she could actually dance with shows a belief in his kindness and warmth.

The black person on the altar may represent persecution. Since the black person appeared in an image with the peacock/Christ, I'll take a wild guess that he represents some form of Christian persecution. The black woman who led her away from the Last Supper was probably the nanny she had had as a child.

This woman is probably looking for more spirituality in her life and is drawn to the kinder aspects of the Christian religion.

These two foregoing cases are examples of how mirror gazing brings out the unconscious, revealing thoughts and feelings that are alive just below the surface. Regular psychotherapy does that too. One advantage of mirror gazing is that it seems to take less time and usually results in a much more visual demonstration of what is going on in the inner reaches of the mind.

GAZING INTO THE UNCONSCIOUS

Mirror gazing may also help psychotherapists find out what is going on in the unconscious minds of people who come to them for help.

Freud believed, and many agree with him, that dreams are "the royal road to the unconscious." He felt that dreams reveal the motivation that exists beneath impulses, actions that our unconscious mind disavows when we are awake.

I feel that mirror visions also give clues to the contents of the unconscious mind. Since the images seen in the speculum are largely creations of the mind of the seer, they constitute what may be called a projective test, somewhat analogous to the famous Rorschach cards, or inkblot test. Such a test might be very helpful in evaluating a client's state of mind.

In my own use of mirror gazing with subjects, I have been able to diagnose a variety of problems, including specific anxieties, depression, and marriage problems.

To do this, I ask the subject to follow a certain procedure, just as the dream-incubation priests in ancient Greece must have done. On the day before the mirror gazing I ask the subjects to frame an idea. For example, if someone is concerned about her relationship with her mother, I ask her to think about her mother at various times during the day. That way, when we finally get down to mirror gazing, the imagery will most likely revolve around the subject of the thoughts. As in dream incubation, images emerge that are more vivid than real life and more symbolic than ordinary thoughts.

Unlike dreams, which are reported to the psychotherapist several hours, if not several days, after the patient has had them and which may not be remembered fully, mirror visions have the potential of being produced by the subject during the actual session, offering access to unconscious material that can be dealt with immediately.

THE ISLAND MAN

One example of this use of mirror gazing as a therapeutic tool occurred with a rough-hewn male student from the rural South. He readily declared that he was not very sophisticated and described his parents as being the same. His mother was a housewife and his father sold insurance.

When we did this gazing session, the man was still living at home. He spoke of his living arrangement with a flat voice, lacking emotion. But at the end of this session he was ready to admit that there were indeed problems at home. Here is what he saw:

I saw a group of people on a beach. They had a fire and were cooking something that looked like fish. I wasn't as interested in the food as I was the people and the place.

We were on an island, and not a very big one at that. I could look up and see the hills on the island behind us. I had a sense that I could walk around this island in no time at all.

We were dressed in very colorful outfits that were made of material that seemed almost like paper. As the people around me walked, the skirts they wore swished like a loose-weave paper. They were very bright colors and clashed greatly with the bright greens of the trees and the sharp reds of the flowers.

In the next scene I was with a bunch of these people and we were running across the shallow parts of the beach, gathering fish that were trapped by the tide. We were happy. There was a lot of fruit on this island, too, all of it sweet and filling.

The feeling among the group was very tribal. There wasn't a feeling that anyone was my mom or dad, but that we were all one with each other. The most amazing thing of all to me was that I couldn't tell if I was male or female. I was just very young.

There was one person that I had a close connection with. He was an old man in the tribe, a cheerful person with a real fat stomach and curly black hair. He was the anchor in my life. I remember sitting by the beach talking with him and feeling very comfortable, but I don't remember what we talked about.

I found it interesting that in the gazing experience he lived on an island and couldn't grow up. When I mentioned this to him, he agreed. It seemed reflective of his current life, in which his parents were anxious and resentful about their son being "out of the nest" and exploring things that they didn't really understand. As he put it, "They are always trying to pull me back into the morass," which to him meant that they are trying to keep him at home as their child.

As we talked, I realized that the old man in the tribe that he felt close to was not his father, whom he did not have much respect for. Nor could it have been either grandfather, since they had both died before he was born. After discussing this point, he concluded that the man on the beach was a kind policeman in his family's community who had been a childhood friend to him.

This single session helped this patient face some problems in his life. Through mirror gazing we were able to get to the heart of a dilemma in his young life. He talked to me a few more times; about the meaning of what he had seen in the crystal and then decided to move out of his parents' house and live on his own.

GAZING AS A DEMONSTRATION TOOL

As a professor of psychology I have found mirror gazing to be a very effective means of demonstrating unconscious mental processes to my students. The purpose of doing this is not to reunite them with dead relatives or even to examine their unconscious feelings. Rather it is to show them that the unconscious mind is active, even when they think it isn't.

I frequently conduct group mirror gazings with my students and have had as many as forty students gazing at one time. Such a class demonstration almost always begins with skepticism. As the gazing session begins, I can hear students gasp at what they are seeing in the reflective surface. By the end of the class time most of the students are agape with wonder at what they have just done and seen. One student said that his experience was "like having a VCR in my head." Another student was astounded that her memories could appear "like three-dimensional movies."

These group mirror gazings always awaken in the students a sense of wonder that energizes them the entire semester. Even though I am accustomed to the mystery of mirror gazing, some of these sessions have produced events that have baffled even me, making me realize that there is much to learn about the unconscious mind.

During one demonstration I had a group of subjects gaze into a speculum. I watched as one of the subjects breathed deeply in order to relax. As he gazed, his eyes grew wider. Later he told me what he had seen:

> I tried to force the visions to come. Then I got frustrated and relaxed. As I did so, I had the experience of suddenly feeling a sort of transference, where I did one hundred and eighty degrees and was sitting in the mirror, staring out at where I had been sitting. I actually felt a rushing feeling, and there I was, in the mirror.
>
> Then the visions came. I remember seeing a field where there was a whole arena of cowboys and Indians. I saw the colors of the war paint and the colors of the clothing. It was a scene in which the

Indians and cowboys were racing across the plains all around me. I was actually "in" the scene.

Where did these images from the American West come from? It was no mystery to the subject who had them. He had been obsessed as a child with the "cowboy culture" of the Old West. All the memories he has of growing up come complete with him wearing a cowboy hat or having a cap gun strapped around his waist.

In light of his fascination with the Wild West, the experience made sense. What baffled him was that his visions were far more realistic than a sleeping dream and even more enjoyable. "I was awake and in the middle of the action," he said. "Sleeping dreams can't top that."

Other things have happened in these classroom demonstrations that were extremely surprising. In one class seven students described the same vision from different parts of the room. Why seven out of thirty people saw a man in a turban I can't begin to answer. Another time two students at different tables saw a ballet dancer in their speculum. Another time a man saw the vision of an inflamed tooth. When he told the class what he had seen, the woman next to him gasped and said that she was having an infected tooth pulled in the morning.

In none of these cases was there any prompting or discussion beforehand that would have led to these images.

The value of these demonstrations is to show psychology students and others that the unconscious is not just some abstraction, but a real level in the human mind that contains our deepest thoughts. By teaching students how to mirror-gaze I can get them to understand this difficult concept. One student said, "I never knew where these images came from until now. I always knew that unconscious images weren't made up. But now I know how real they are."

A RIVER OF KNOWLEDGE

William James called the subconscious mind "a river, forever flowing through a man's conscious waking hours." This description is awe-inspiring when we realize how little we know about the content of that river. Perhaps it is mirror gazing, with its ability to tap into this invisible river of knowledge, that can make our deepest thoughts and most forgotten memories visible. If that is the case, then it can be used as a tool for psychological exploration that can greatly reduce the amount of time a person may need to spend with an analyst.

SIX

CREATING YOUR OWN PSYCHOMANTEUM

A lake is the first and most expressive feature of a landscape. It is the eye of the earth, where the spectator, looking at it with his own, sounds the depth of his own nature.

—Henry David Thoreau

Mirror gazing is a form of self-exploration. And as with any exploration, one needs to be in the right mood and have the proper equipment before a satisfying journey is possible.

My special setting for mirror gazing replicates settings of psychomanteums down through history. It has been clear since the time of very early man that the control of these visions relies on the creation of a unique environment, one that is completely set apart from the everyday world, so that the drama of the unconscious mind can be brought to the surface.

This need for a special setting is what led the keepers of the psychomanteum at Ephyra to create a complex of subterranean structures. It was in this maze of caves and barely lit rooms that the unconscious mind became visible when the apparition seekers were finally led into the apparitional chamber and were allowed to gaze into the polished cauldron filled with water.

The house in which John Dee communed with angels was specially equipped with a room that can best be described as an apparitional chamber. It was comfortable and dimly lit, and it incorporated a variety of specula, from Dee's famous obsidian mirror to ordinary mirrors. Dee's chamber was like the many that came before. All the apparition seekers in all the cultures between the Greeks and Elizabethan England conducted their attempts to raise spirits in carefully planned and equipped rooms.

The architects and operators of all those facilities knew something that has become obvious to me too. They realized that such spiritually pregnant and emotionally laden encounters should take place in an environment assembled in accordance with certain physical, psychological and aesthetic principles. It should be this way for at least two reasons:

- It is fitting and appropriate that a person undergoing a transformative spiritual experience do so in a setting that is memorably pleasant and uplifting.
- Features of an environment can be arranged so as

to precipitate altered states of awareness in the people being exposed to it.

These two factors are illustrated by the Greeks, who built their Oracle centers at impressive locations that were also considered to be places where this world touched the next. The Oracle at Ephyra for instance, was believed to be located near the entrance to the Underworld.

At Ephyra the required interdimensional effect was achieved by harmonizing numerous known ways of altering consciousness with a single unified space. The subterranean location of the facility, for example, was sufficient to create an atmosphere that had a strange effect upon the psyche. By the same token the two African groups who resorted to mirror gazing had methods of altering consciousness: the Nkomis used sensory deprivation and social isolation; the Bwiti cult used sleep deprivation and intoxication. All three used mirror gazing as the means of seeing the spirits.

CREATING THE MOOD

I decided to employ a multimodal approach in designing my latter-day psychomanteum, taking special care to acknowledge the kinship between play and the para-normal. I encourage laughter as an integral part of my program, but not to coerce participants into an attitude of frivolity or hilarity. Rather the aim is to allow them safely and comfortably to surrender some of their inhibitions, thereby enhancing their chances of entering into an altered state of consciousness. By looking at comedies on videocassettes or even reading comic books, patients are not making light of the experience they are about to have, which is conjuring the spirit of a departed relative. No, what they are doing is making it easier to accept what is about to happen. In that sense humor is the gateway to the paranormal for some people.

My strategy has also been to incorporate within this environment as many as possible of the factors known to ease the transition into altered states of awareness. In addition to humor, these factors include: nature, alterations in the sense of time, art, and intellectual stimulation—and, of course, crystalline surfaces such as mirrors.

I have already mentioned in an earlier chapter the ways in which I incorporated all of these factors into the Theater of the Mind. But if you are wondering just how you would create the mood that is necessary to facilitate apparitions if you were to attempt mirror gazing on your own; let me review each of these components and offer some suggestions.

Nature   Since the Theater of the Mind is located in a rural area of the Deep South, I have no problem steeping my subjects in a relaxing natural environment. We are surrounded by forest and farmlands that are pleasant to walk in. The creek that runs by my converted gristmill is filled with turtles and snakes and provides the soothing sound of rushing water.

In more urban settings nature is hard to find. If that is

the case where you live, you might try artificial means of duplicating nature. Most nature stores carry a selection of audiotapes of nature sounds. These include the sounds of waves lapping the shore or rain in a tropical forest. By listening to these tapes on a Walkman while strolling through a park or even along a city street, I have found that they help achieve the deep relaxation I am seeking.

Alterations in the sense of time   At the Theater of the Mind subjects are asked not to wear watches. They are also surrounded by an antique decor that includes no clocks. The point of this is to propel them back to an earlier era, a time when people relied less on technology. Such surroundings give us a sense of history, reminding us of generations that have come and gone before. They also remind us that people got along fine in a slower environment.

If you don't already have many antique pieces of furniture or a room devoted to antiques, I suggest establishing this mood by looking at a book of old photographs or illustrations of life in an earlier time. If you really want to be propelled backward in time, search an antiques store for a stereoscopic viewer and the cards that go with it This forgotten method of looking at photographs puts you through a kind of window into a time long past.

Covering the faces of any existing clocks is also important, both to further the illusion of reuniting with the past and to short-circuit the modern awareness of time. If it is necessary to keep track of the passage of time,

I suggest timing the mirror-gazing sessions by means of an hourglass, an archaic but effective method.

Art Art alone is enough to induce altered states in many people. I mentioned the Stendhal syndrome earlier, the form of nervous breakdown suffered by many who are exposed to great art. I also said that some musicians have reported paranormal experiences, including the sensation of being out-of-body while performing great musical masterpieces.

In light of this I have made use of both music and art to open people's minds to this altered consciousness. Art is displayed throughout the building, and not just "pretty" art. Art is chosen that is surprising, shocking, funny, disturbing—all aimed at stimulating the brain in ways it is not accustomed to.

These effects of art are not difficult to create at home. It could be done by changing the types of art you may have hanging on your walls now. Or without going to that expense or trouble you could peruse art books and get the same effect. The works of Salvador Dali, Max Ernst and Pablo Picasso are readily available in colorful picture books and have a way of stimulating most people. I also find cartoon art to be particularly enlivening, especially the work of Carl Barks, the artist who drew Donald Duck's Uncle Scrooge.

To be soothed by beauty is only part of the rationale of using art to prepare yourself for mirror gazing. To be surprised, shocked and even feel a sense of displacement is important. Also, aesthetic appreciation is itself a kind of altered sense of awareness. The effect we are after is novel stimulation that will give you a sense of wonder about the world of perception.

Intellectual stimulation The pursuit of knowledge has always been an important channel through which human beings have sought spiritual direction and enlightenment. As I said earlier, I maintain an extensive library at the Theater of the Mind filled with books on altered states of consciousness, the paranormal, and spirituality. You can easily do the same at home, since most of these books are available at large bookstores.

I don't think intellectual stimulation comes only from books. Since mirror gazing is visual, some find it preferable to get their intellectual stimulation from a visual medium, especially one that allows them the opportunity to let their minds wander.

Spending some time looking through a microscope is one way of doing this. I have recently installed an easy-to-use dissecting microscope so that my subjects can take a mind-bending excursion into the microcosmic realms.

The macrocosmic realm has possibilities too. An astronomer recently told me of a report in an astronomy journal about the large number of astronomers who have out-of-body experiences or other profound inner adventures while peering through their telescopes across vast interplanetary and interstellar expanses.

This only indicates to me the mind-expanding nature of the universe around us and the magical ways that close contact with it can affect our senses.

Mementos Finally, if you are attempting to see a departed loved one, it is important to imprint that person firmly in your mind. Doing so shouldn't be too difficult. Photographs are the most effective way I have found to do this. A family album filled with great memories stirs up the conscious as well as the unconscious mind. Family films and videos do the same thing.

Another way to inspire sentiment about a departed loved one is through mementos. I have had people bring articles of clothing associated with the person. They have also brought fishing poles, woodworking tools, chess sets, pipes, glasses, old letters, and so on. Anything associated with that person is an effective way of bringing up memories and feelings.

COMBINING THESE FACTORS

The purpose of all these factors is to reduce the level of inhibitions you might have over mirror gazing as well as establish a mood that will make it easier to enter the mind's other dimensions.

I would like to be able to offer specific guidelines as to how long you should spend with each of the above disciplines, but I can't. For some people an hour spent communing with nature would be too long, while a half hour spent looking at old photographs would be too short. When I am conducting one of these sessions, I can generally tell from the subject's level of enthusiasm when it is time to move on.

My advice to you in trying this on your own is simple:

Don't bore yourself. If fifteen minutes of looking at art feels like enough to you, then it is. If you want to walk in nature for an hour, then by all means do it. The same is true of mementos. If looking at old photos for half an hour feels like enough, then it probably is. As long as you are stimulated and not bored by what you are doing, then all is well.

The state of mind associated with seeing the visions is a subtle one. Maintaining an attitude of tense expectancy definitely seems to block the experience. On the other hand, quietly and confidently assuming that the apparitions will appear seems to increase the likelihood that they will. The operating factor here seems to be a state of relaxation.

Once you have completed all of these steps and feel prepared, you can move on to the actual mirror gazing itself.

THE SPECULUM

A wide variety of objects have been used for gazing. Several are mentioned in this book, including crystal balls; mirrors; polished metal; bowls or cups filled with water, ink, blood, or wine; polished lamps; lakes; and so forth. Almost anything that affords a clear depth has possibilities when it comes to mirror gazing.

In earlier times people assumed that mirror visions were produced by magical powers inherent in the speculum itself. Such belief persists even today. From time to time I have heard salesmen in crystal shops intimate that real quartz crystal balls are better for gazing because they contain magical powers.

In general the various substances used as media for gazing may well call up different emotional associations. Hence, hydromancy, which has been a common form of mirror gazing throughout the ages, calls forth the mythology related to water, which is one of the most common symbols of the unconscious mind. Crystal on the other hand, is a common unconscious image of the self. And stones, which are sometimes polished and used for gazing, conjure an unconscious image of permanence. They are also linked with humankind's spiritual and intellectual quests: Christ was said to have built his church on a rock, Muslims visit the sacred stone at Mecca, the Rosetta stone was the key that unlocked the secrets of ancient tongues, and John Dee referred to his obsidian speculum as the holy stone.

In this sense there may be some significance to the type of speculum chosen. Indeed specula often become symbols of the "self." Kenneth MacKenzie, the fifteenth-century Scottish crystal gazer, claimed that his gazing stone was dropped on his chest while he slept. John Dee claims that his "shew stone" came to him in the midst of a visitation by angels. Many contemporary mirror gazers have given similar accounts of how they obtained their specula.

Objects that reflect the inner being can actually become treated as a part of the being. In fact, the deeper the search for self, the more likely this is to occur. It becomes a symbol of the quest for self-knowledge. One more piece of evidence that the crystal ball is seen as a symbol of self comes to us from humorists, who say that the crystal ball is "defective" when the fortune-teller they are consulting sees an image that they don't like.

Ultimately it is the mind of the gazer and not any occult essence of the speculum that is the basis for mirror visions. The crystal medium is in effect a mirror of the soul. That we are not fully aware of this fact while mirror gazing is one factor that lends an uncanny atmosphere to the entire experience. Processes within the mind are invested with an aura of mystery by being given an apparent spatial location within the speculum itself.

All things considered, I think it is important to use a speculum with which you feel truly comfortable. I prefer using a mirror. You may prefer one of the other media mentioned. It doesn't matter which one you use. It only matters that it works.

THE ACT OF GAZING

Make sure that no one disturbs you during your mirror-gazing session. Find a private spot; unplug the telephone; you might even hang a DO NOT DISTURB sign on your door if necessary. It is important that you find a comfortable place where you can truly relax.

Posture is important. Sit in a comfortable chair that will support the back of your head, even if you are deeply relaxed. Arrange your chair and the mirror medium so that you can gaze into it without having to hold your eyes at an uncomfortable angle.

Dim light from behind usually works the best, although you will have to experiment until you get the lighting just right. I have found that it helps to use candlelight or an electric candlestick, especially at first. It is also felt that the best time for mirror gazing is in the twilight hours, a time that seems to inspire altered states in many people. Later, when you become more proficient, you will find that mirror gazing is possible even in bright lights.

The technique for mirror gazing itself is remarkably easy. Seat yourself comfortably, relax and gaze into the clear depth of the speculum without trying to see anything. Some compare this to looking off into the distance. Properly relaxed, your arms will feel very heavy and the tips of your fingers will tingle as though charged slightly by electricity. This tingling feeling almost always signals the beginning of the hypnagogic state.

The speculum will most likely become cloudy now. Some people report an image that resembles the sky on a cloudy day. Others say that the mirror becomes darker. Whatever the case, this change in the clarity of the speculum signals to you that the visions are about to appear.

LET IT FLOW

People often ask whether it is better to pose a particular question when the visions appear or whether it is best to watch them unfold passively. As a general rule I feel that you should not direct the experience at first. Instead just let the images flow.

Attempting to guide the images adds a further layer of

complications that decrease the likelihood that one will see images in the speculum. After you have become more adept at mirror gazing; putting specific questions into your mind *before* entering the trance state can be very helpful, especially if your object is self-exploration or self-understanding. Attempting to direct images *after* they have begun will usually cause them to fade away. Why this happens I am not sure, but my guess is that conscious thought brings you out of the hypnagogic state of mind where these images occur.

How long do the images last? Usually less than a minute, especially for those unable to stay relaxed. Some of my subjects have been able to maintain images for as long as ten minutes on their first attempt. The more proficient you become at mirror gazing, the longer you will see images on the speculum.

Sometimes you may see nothing yet hear the departed person talk or feel his or her touch. Some may experience all the sensations of a given person or location without actually seeing anything. And, as you know from reading this book, you may have the sensation of passing into the speculum, or the images may actually come out with you. Whatever the case, it will be obvious when the visionary experience starts and when it is over.

KEEP A RECORD OF THE EXPERIENCE

I recommend that you record the experience immediately after the session. Write it down in as much detail as possible. Include the sensations leading up to the visionary experience, what you saw or sensed while you were having the experience, and what happened to make you come out of it.

Careful record keeping will help you know what to expect the next time you mirror-gaze. It will also show differences between sessions and will eventually let you know how to get the most out of your mirror-gazing experience.

Recording your experiences will also help you remember them as they really were. Write down the nature of your vision, including what or whom you saw and heard and even how you felt as events unfolded. Doing this will give you a way to recall the precise experience later.

DON'T TRY TOO HARD

If the visions do not occur during a session, then it is necessary to consider some of the possible factors involved.

The most common reason for failing to see anything is trying too hard. Subjects sometimes report that the visions miraculously begin after they give up, or at least after they entertain thoughts of doing so.

I once conducted a workshop with eight people, all of whom happened to be recovering alcoholics. Only two of them experienced any visions at all during the mirror-gazing session. As a possible reason for this they mentioned that alcoholics are "control freaks" and as a result couldn't relax and let their minds wander. I suggested that the next time they simply "give up" and then sit there awhile longer since the very idea of quitting could relax them.

In some ways the state of mind for visionary experience is the opposite of the state of mind we are in when we are consciously trying to do something. Yet at the same time, maintaining an attitude of confident expectation also helps the images to come. The operative factor here seems to be a state of mental relaxation.

Distractions are another common reason that visions fail to take place. These can include outside noise and physical discomfort. Perhaps the room is too hot or too cold, or maybe it is just too noisy. Distractions also take place in the form of diet. Some people simply cannot have visionary experiences after eating a heavy meal, though a light one is recommended since it elevates your blood sugar and keeps you from focusing on your hunger. And some cannot mirror-gaze successfully when they have ingested caffeine since this common stimulant can make people too nervous. Connection has also been made between a diet high in potassium and effective imagery. On the other hand, those who consume large amounts of calcium tend not to experience visions as readily. The message here is to eat more fruit and vegetables and fewer dairy products the day before mirror gazing.

I also want to emphasize that exercise is an important component of relaxation. Most people are far more relaxed after even gentle exercise and have the lower blood pressure and slower heart rate to prove it. If you are having difficulty relaxing or letting your mind wander while mirror gazing, it might be due to a lack of exercise.

Exercise is one of the best ways I have found to inspire the deep muscle relaxation that facilitates entrance into the visionary state. Of course, check with your physician before starting an exercise program.

Another reason that some people fail to see visions is physical pain. Back pain particularly can make it difficult for some people to sit up, let alone relax and mirror-gaze. If that is the case, then there is nothing wrong with lying down and mirror gazing.

Sometimes it just takes a long time or many attempts to have a successful visionary experience. You may be completely at ease with the process and still have no visions. I invite you to persevere and to try it several times. In my experience a little more than half the people who try it have a vision the first time. Quite a few of the rest will have a vision on the second, third, or even fourth attempt.

Why do people try again after failing the first time? The answer is probably found in the other pleasures of mirror gazing. Most people say they have never felt so relaxed before in their whole life. Some even mirror-gaze primarily for the relaxation, considering the visions an interesting by-product.

KEEP IT PLAYFUL

If all of this seems more like play than science, then I have accomplished my goal.

Somewhere along the line, parapsychology has become abstract and intellectualized and seems almost to have renounced its connection to the soul. It tries to be a serious science, so it often fails to console those who look to it in times of personal loss and sorrow.

In one style in which it is pursued, parapsychology bears a resemblance to science. I submit that it also bears a resemblance to entertainment, humor and play.

While dour types downplay their importance, humor and play are among the most significant of human enterprises. The consolation they offer can be indispensable in facing life, not to mention the fact that creative play is an important wellspring of discovery.

Parapsychology at its best can awaken us to the uncanny nature of the universe in which we live and to the continuing wonder of the consciousness with which we experience that universe.

In effect, parapsychology orchestrates certain methods or techniques of systematic inquiry in order to serve a spiritual end. It can stir profound emotions of awe and amazement. Although it cannot offer us proof of life after death, it can allow us hope.

I do not mean in any way to suggest that parapsychologists (which includes you as you mirror-gaze) are willing to make do with any less than an exacting respect for the truth. You must love the truth as deeply as do scientists, although you cannot conduct the same systematic search for it that scientists do.

FINDING THE BOUNDARIES

The intended effect of the interplay of all these elements in mirror gazing is to create a doorway to other dimensions of the mind. Thus it comes as a pleasant confirmation to hear visitors compare this to "stepping into another world."

People following the techniques I have developed have regularly reported striking manifestations of phenomena that have traditionally been described as paranormal. Yet all of this has been achieved through an approach that makes no claims whatsoever about the metaphysical status of these experiences.

Subjects are encouraged to decide for themselves as to the reality and significance of their experiences. It is within this environment—one that you can easily create at home—that you can take voyages to the farthest reaches of human consciousness.

SEVEN

FUTURE USES OF MIRROR GAZING

The subliminal life has windows of outlook and doors of ingress which indefinitely extend the region of the world of truth.

—William James

A number of potential values and applications of mirror gazing come readily to mind. These applications may result in a richer understanding of the capacities and limitations of the human mind. But beyond their psychological implications, mirror gazing may lead to a deeper understanding of history and literature.

First let's examine the role of mirror gazing in human psychology.

Perhaps most important to those who study the mind is the possibility that mirror gazing may open a portal into an altered state of awareness. If facilitated apparitions of the departed prove to be indistinguishable from spontaneous ones, then a common phenomenon that has long been assumed by many to be paranormal has at last become

168

available for study under controlled circumstances.

By "study" I don't mean just gathering stories from people who have had these experiences. I mean that mirror gazing may well finally allow these altered states to be studied in a laboratory setting. This would represent a major leap forward in psychology. It would mean that subjects could be interviewed immediately after—or even during—an altered state.

Electroencephalograms and positron emission tomography could be carried out during an apparitional experience so that science could finally make maps of the metabolic activity in the brain that occurs during these encounters.

Since it has been impossible to investigate these altered states in a laboratory, many skeptics have said that those who have paranormal experiences as well as those who research them tend to "overstate" what happens, or even that the experiences themselves are fabricated by the subjects. This uninformed opinion rarely takes into consideration the sheer masses of people who see ghosts, or have near-death experiences, or even leave their bodies. Although we are talking about literally millions of people in these three categories alone, some cynics call them liars or crackpots, denying an experience that was real to the subject.

PLACE-BOUND EXPLANATIONS

By facilitating apparitions in psychomanteums we may also be able to explain "place-bound" apparitions. These are apparitions that haunt a specific place. Sometimes these hauntings can go on for centuries, especially if the area is undisturbed. Some of the most famous place-bound hauntings occur in European castles, old cathedrals and churches and wilderness areas. Place-bound apparitions are often the result of sudden death, murder, or some other violent death.

The following is typical of the place-bound apparitions reported to researchers; it comes from the files of Gardner Murphy and Herbert Klemme:

On October 3, 1963, Mrs. Coleen Buterbaugh, secretary to Dean Sam Dahl, of Nebraska Wesleyan University, Lincoln, Nebraska, was asked by Dean Dahl to take a message to a colleague, Professor Martin (pseudonym), in his office suite in the C. C. White Building nearby. At about 8:50 A.M. Mrs. Buterbaugh entered this building and walked briskly along its extensive hall, hearing the sounds of students in a group of rooms set aside for music practice, and notably a marimba playing. Entering the first room of the suite, she took about four steps and was stopped short by a very intense odor—a musty, disagreeable odor. Raising her eyes, she saw the figure of a very tall, black-haired woman in a shirtwaist and ankle-length skirt who was extending her right arm to the upper right-hand shelves in an old music cabinet. We now continue the account in Mrs. Buterbaugh's own words:

"As I first walked into the room everything was

quite normal. About four steps into the room was when the strong odor hit me. When I say strong odor, I mean the kind that simply stops you in your tracks and almost chokes you. I was looking down at the floor, as one often does when walking, and as soon as that odor stopped me I felt that there was someone in the room with me. It was then that I was aware that there were no noises out in the hall. Everything was deathly quiet. I looked up and something drew my eyes to the cabinet along the wall in the next room. I looked up and there she was. She had her back to me, reaching up into one of the shelves of the cabinet with her right hand, and standing perfectly still. She wasn't at all aware of my presence. While I was watching her she never moved. She was not transparent and yet I knew she wasn't real. While I was looking at her she just faded away—not parts of her body one at a time, but her whole body all at once.

"Up until the time she faded away I was not aware of anyone else being in the suite of rooms, but just about the time of her fading out I felt as though I was still not alone. To my left was a desk and I had a feeling there was a man sitting at that desk. I turned around and saw no one, but I still felt his presence. When that feeling of his presence left I have no idea, because it was then, when I looked out the window behind that desk, that I got frightened and left the room I am not sure whether I ran or walked out of the room. When I looked out that window there wasn't even one modern thing out there. The street, which is less than half a block away from the building, was not even there and neither was the new Willard House. That was when I realized that these people were not in my time, but that I was back in their time."

What are these place-bound apparitions all about? Why is the same ghost seen by many different people, even those who know nothing about the history of an area nor the fact that it is "haunted"?

Using visionary facilitation may make it possible to put these questions to a test, providing answers that have long evaded researchers.

COLLECTIVE APPARITIONS

An extension of the present method should make it possible to facilitate collective apparitions among several subjects at once, all trying to facilitate an apparition of the same deceased person. Spontaneous collective mirror apparitions of the departed have been documented, and the accounts of ancient Greeks imply that they took place in the psychomanteums. This gives me confidence that this line of investigation will eventually come to fruition.

I will leave this line of inquiry to other researchers. I happen to be better at one-on-one interactions. As a result I am not going to pursue this line of research. I am hopeful that colleagues who are more proficient at conducting group sessions will carry out this project.

Success in that endeavor may well tell us something about the dynamics of collective visionary phenomena.

GRIEF THERAPY

The study of facilitated apparitions may also yield insight into the psychology of bereavement. It is well known that people in the throes of grief often become preoccupied with images of the deceased. They may carry around photographs of lost loved ones, gazing at them with great frequency. If one conceptualizes apparitions of the departed as an aspect of the mind's ability, then this work may help us better understand the grieving process—and for that matter reduce the pain of grief.

It is common for those who spontaneously experience apparitions of deceased loved ones to have a reduction, even complete resolution, of their grief. This is quite consistent with the outcomes described by subjects who encountered the departed in the psychomanteum. Many of these people considered the event to be a healing of their relationships with lost loved ones.

PSYCHOLOGY OF HISTORY

For my part I plan to continue my research along several lines of inquiry. I am in the process of locating historical material that will aid in the study of the classical oracles of the dead. I will visit these sites in hopes of better understanding the environment and methods used by the ancients to conjure the dead.

For example, most people who hear for the first time about shamanism assume that the shamans were either charlatans, mentally ill, or that they possessed some extraordinary faculty that most of us lack. We have already seen that shamans claimed to be able to take voyages into the spirit world through their magic mirrors, where they then saw spirits of the dead. As you now know from this book, the inner world of those ancient tribal practitioners is accessible to us all.

These ancient rites are made more understandable when one is familiar with mirror gazing. This knowledge casts light on the lives of many individual historical figures. We also have a better grasp of some of the central institutions of ancient Greece.

We are also helped to understand the ways in which visionary states can enhance creativity. It is now clear that Thomas Edison was using the hypnagogic state to explore his unconscious mind for many of the inventions that changed the course of modern man. The same can be said for other great scientists, inventors, and thinkers. That these marvels of the unconscious mind have happened with these great men of history is an indication that they may have happened in other cases and can most likely be made to happen again.

SAD STORY OF THE XHOSAS

History shows us how this phenomenon may result in chilling events when it erupts unexpectedly into a culture that is not prepared to understand it. You may find it incomprehensible that some people would become so obsessed with mirror visions that they could actually begin to rule their lives. But such things have happened in history, the most recent being the national suicide of the Xhosa people of South Africa.

The many well-documented accounts of this nineteenth-century tragedy describe the spontaneous emergence of a psychomanteum into a primitive culture. The results gave rise to an obsession with mirror visions that led to unrealistic expectations and escapism of the highest order.

The Xhosas were a demoralized people. They had fought wars with European colonists since 1778 and had fought half a dozen more wars with the British in the first half of the 1800s.

Their Stone Age weapons were no match for the superior firepower of the Europeans. They met with defeat in all of their battles. The most humiliating defeat of all came during the war of 1850, which lasted three years and left sixteen thousand Xhosas dead.

The British weren't content to stop with victory. One colonial governor forced some of the Xhosa chieftains to kiss his boot as a sign of defeat.

The one area in which the Xhosas were able to maintain their pride was in their cattle. They were excellent herdsmen who respected and treasured their cattle. There were times when they even worshiped them in special ceremonies. Cattle were given individual names and were a popular subject of Xhosa poetry and songs. The Xhosa men identified themselves with their favorite animals in much the way that American men identify themselves with their automobiles. There was a difference: the livelihood of the Xhosa people relied upon their cattle. Without them they would die.

On an autumn evening in 1856 a young girl named Nongquase ran breathless into camp and reported seeing ten black strangers in a pool next to a river. Since her uncle was the tribe's most eminent shaman and prophet, her vision was thought to have special meaning.

In short order her uncle went to the river himself and saw the men at the pool. He was astounded to see his own deceased brother among the group. A spokesman told him that they were messengers from the beyond and that they had things to tell him. Then they disappeared.

During the next few weeks Nongquase was sent to the pool repeatedly, where she conversed with the mirror beings while standing waist deep in the water. Word of the miracle spread, and soon the young prophet and her uncle were guiding Xhosa tribal chieftains through the experience. Some saw visions of their own.

At last Kreli, the great king of the Xhosas, came to the pool to see for himself what was happening. He, too, soon had a powerful vision of his departed son. It was as though the boy was brought back to life, he said later.

King Kreli was profoundly moved by the experience. He became a proponent of the prophecies from the pool, even the ones that called for the killing of the cattle so that the ancestors could rise from the dead.

Not everyone agreed with these prophecies, especially those in distant Xhosaland, where the people felt slighted by the fact that the ancestors had elected to appear at a site so far from their villages. They made it known that they wanted to see their departed relatives locally.

Nine months later that happened. The eleven-year-old daughter of a local shaman began to visit with mirror entities at a pool near her village. She claimed to have encounters with the spirit of a departed Xhosa who had been much loved among his people. She heard him talking. He said the spirits would come back to life if the cattle were killed.

It was in this atmosphere that the great cattle killing began. Soon carcasses of dead animals littered the landscape. The British colonial officials tried to stop the madness by arresting the visionaries, but it was too late. The mass starvation that followed decimated the Xhosa people, and no departed souls emerged as promised.

The British authorities did not understand the psychology behind the phenomenon that had touched off the cattle slaying. But we now know that the combination of visionary facilitation and low self-esteem spelled disaster for this ancient people.

But the plight of the Xhosas should remind us to keep mirror-gazing activity from shading into cult activity. Thoughtful analysis can keep visionary experiences in their place, keeping it as a way of helping human beings instead of becoming a reason for being.

ALTERED STATES AND HISTORY

It is plain that altered states of consciousness can have the effect of awakening an interest in history, of inspiring a new way of understanding it, or even, in the case of Arnold Toynbee, of inducing someone to write a study of it.

In Volume Ten of his monumental A *Study of History*, Toynbee devotes a chapter to events that inspired historians to write their best works. Most of the historians he discusses were led to their interest in history by the great wars. But he and Edward Gibbon were among the notable exceptions who were inspired by visionary experiences. For Gibbon, who wrote *The Decline and Fall of the Roman Empire*, his mystical moment came while sitting on the steps of the Temple of Jupiter listening to barefoot Mars chant their litanies. Suddenly the modern city changed to the ruins of the ancient city and back again. The vision of physical decay led him to trace the fall of what was possibly history's greatest empire. In summing up Gibbon's experience, Toynbee describes beautifully the nature of such experiences:

This imaginative experience was the sole flash of inspiration with which Gibbon was ever visited. Without it, that wonderful genius might never have come to flower, and that famous name might have found no place in the record of Mankind's intellectual history. In chronological terms the psychic event which had these momentous consequences may have occupied no more than a fraction of one second out of the thirty-six years or so of the great historian's adult intellectual life; yet his watchful muse did not fail to see and seize her fleeting opportunity of gaining access to a mind which was

178

normally rendered impervious to her divine promptings by a carapace of innate scepticism that had been case-hardened in an all too congenial eighteen-century Western mental climate.

Toynbee then writes of his own visionary experience, one that took place in the twilight hours, when he was sitting on a hillside overlooking Sparta after an exhausting day of hiking. As he pondered the city on the hill before him, he began to wonder if there had been a city there before this one. Biblical passages came to mind, such as "A city that is set on a hill cannot be hid" and "I will lift up mine eyes unto the hills, from whence cometh my help."

Suddenly, wrote Toynbee, speaking of himself in the third person, "the gazer saw staring him in the face, on the crown of the bluff that overhung the farther bank of the Eurotas just opposite the all but coincident sites of Sparta the First and Sparta the Second, a monument that signalled to him the location of the pre-Hellenic counterpart of the Frankish and Ottomon citadel over whose battlements he was looking out."

Toynbee seemed to have a glimpse—even a trip—into the past. He cherished this vision. Indeed he even claims that he might not have produced his monumental *Study of History* without having had this experience. As he wrote (referring to himself in the third person), Toynbee might not have produced his volumes of history "if this synoptic view had not unfolded itself physically before his eyes from the summit of Mistra on the 23rd May, 1912, in an experience that had been personal to the spectator."

It is conceivable that mirror visions could be used to elucidate the way historians study and write history. Many authors engrossed in the detail of historical figures say that they are haunted by the presence of their subjects.

These facts hint to me that historical personages could be "visited" by biographers under the controlled circumstances of the psychomanteum. It is possible that the interplay of conscious and unconscious factors could add historical understanding.

This may seem outlandish at first mention, but the account of Toynbee shows the relevance of the unconscious mind and altered states of awareness to the ways in which history is studied.

Even Toynbee agrees. He acknowledges the contributions of Carl Jung's work to his own study of history, declaring:

C. G. Jung . . . opened up for me a new dimension in the realm of Life. The admirable catholicity with which Jung draws upon materials of the most diverse kinds for the illustration of his themes enabled me to find my way into the terra incognita of the psyche's subconscious abyss by proceeding from the known to the unknown. . . . The re-emergence, after a submarine voyage, of splinters of conscious psychic life that have been submerged in the Subconscious was the equivalent of the re-emergence. . . .

Toynbee praised Plato in the same way, stating that Plato instructed future historians to take what they know is true and venture into the world of imagination. As he wrote so eloquently:

> Plato taught me, by example, not to be ashamed of using my imagination as well as my intellect. He taught me, when, in a mental voyage, I found myself at the upper limit of the atmosphere accessible to the Reason, not to hesitate to let my imagination carry me on up into the stratosphere on the wings of a myth. . . . Plato's example . . . had given me courage to part company with an early-twentieth-century Western Zeitgeist whose oracles were scales and dividers because, in this Geist's self-blinkered eyes, the only realities were those that could be weighed and measured.

I urge any historian to attempt a mirror vision who is interested in such an opportunity. Such a voyage from the known into the unknown would surely have interesting results. It may also have value in making connections and tying up loose ends concerning events that have eluded traditional methods of research.

The unconscious mind is a powerful tool for understanding. In this mysterious region of the mind, problems are solved and events clarified long before they enter consciousness. To be able to tap into such a rich mother lode of information in so dramatic a way as mirror gazing surely holds a great potential for those wanting to connect with the past.

LITERARY IMPLICATIONS

Up until now no one has quite understood how such fantastical stories could spring up in a given culture. But in the light of present knowledge it is clear that elements of mirror vision play an important role in many myths, legends, fairy tales, superstitions, religious practices, historical events, and even personal voyages. Following is a summary of the elements contained in many of these stories:

The presence of a reflective surface or object   Lludd's cauldron, the fisherman's copper bottle, Odysseus' trench of blood, Dr. Dee's obsidian mirror—all represent a reflective surface that provides the possibility for mirror vision.

This surface, or speculum, may be characterized as being special or even magical   For example, Kenneth MacKenzie of Scotland awoke one afternoon from a nap to find a gazing stone resting on his chest. He said that the stone had been placed there by angels and considered it his most cherished speculum.

A magical or ritualistic act may be required to prime the speculum and awaken its powers   The literature of myth is filled with examples of this. One of the best-known examples is Snow White's evil stepmother, who chants, "Mirror, mirror on the wall, who is the fairest of them all?" before her magic mirror divulges its judgment. Aladdin, too, must polish the surface of his lamp before its shiny, clear depth reveals the genie.

Ritual has always played a strong role in mirror visions. There is no doubt that cleaning a surface will make it a shinier and better speculum, but the purpose of ritual in mirror gazing is also to prepare the subject to have a vision. By following age-old rituals, subjects are convinced that they have earned a vision.

An entity of some kind is associated with the speculum
There is almost always some kind of spirit—be it evil or kind—present in the speculum. We see this throughout myth and literature as well as in real life. I have had subjects who have had apparitions come out of the mirror and visit them.

Most popular in myth is the entity in the evil witch's mirror who delivers the bad news that Snow White is the fairest woman in the land. He is immediately smashed, broken into a thousand pieces, for delivering this harsh bit of truth. Aladdin's genie pops out of the lamp, too, as do the dragons in Lludd's Celtic tale.

A human may enter into the mirror realm   As we now know from my experimentation, it is not uncommon for a human being to enter the mirror realm through the speculum.

Such a phenomenon explains the fantastic voyage that Alice took in Lewis Carroll's *Through the Looking Glass*. It also provides an explanation for the somewhat hoary experience Odysseus had as he gazed into the spirit world through a shimmering pool of blood.

The examples of this in literature often seem fanciful or incomprehensible. By understanding that such trans-ference is a part of mirror gazing, it becomes clear that such experiences have played a role in literature.

This interface between the ordinary world and the realm inhabited by mirror beings can be hazardous for humans and mirror folk alike. Since the genie in the bottle has murder on his mind when he is released, the fisherman must trick him in order to get him back into the bottle. On the other hand, the dragons get drunk on mead in the Celtic tale and are trapped *outside* the mirror. The story of Numa's nymph represents an inbetween fate in that she was transformed into the very fountain from which she came.

In real life there have been hazards for mirror gazers as well. Their dangers didn't come from inside the mirror but from the people around them. John Dee was hounded by accusations of sorcery throughout his long life. Cagliostro was considered a charlatan by some (as he may well have been). And poor Kenneth MacKenzie was buried headfirst in boiling tar for telling a queen the truth about her philandering husband, whom he saw with another woman in his mirror speculum.

Death and mourning play a large role in these legends
As in real-life visionary facilitation, death, mourning, and bereavement loom large in most of these narratives. Aladdin's father had died, as had Snow White's real mother. Odysseus sailed to Ephyra immediately after the death of his comrade, Elpenor. While gazing into a pool

of blood, he discovered that his mother, Anticleia, had passed away in his absence.

Once again myth and reality come together, since mourning plays a powerful role in why real people seek mirror visions. And as with some of the mythical figures, real people are healed of their grief by seeing departed loved ones.

There is a focus on marital separation, domestic disharmony, or social disturbance Odysseus journeys to the Oracle of the Dead at Ephyra to see whether he will be able to go back home to his wife, Penelope. Snow White's stepmother envied the young woman's beauty and was trying to murder her. And Aladdin's family was surely disturbed by the genie in the lamp.

THE RIDDLE OF PANDORA'S BOX SOLVED

Perhaps one of the most mysterious of all myths, Pandora's Box, may now be illuminated by mirror visions.

In the legend of Pandora that we are most familiar with, the earth's first woman opens a box that releases plagues of all sorts on mankind. We say that it was a box because we follow the rewriting of the tale by the fourteenth-century scholar Erasmus of Rotterdam.

In the story's earliest account, that of the Greek poet Hesiod, however, Pandora did not have a box. Rather, all the spirits emerged from a specific type of jar known as a *pithos*. This was a large container used for a variety of purposes. Here is the story as told in *Bulfinch's Mythology*:

> The first woman was named Pandora. She was made in heaven, every god contributing something to perfect her. Venus gave her beauty, Mercury persuasion, Apollo music, etc. Thus equipped, she was conveyed to earth, and presented to Epimetheus, who gladly accepted her, though cautioned by his brother to beware of Jupiter and his gifts. Epimetheus had in his house a jar, in which were kept certain noxious articles for which, in fitting man for his new abode, he had had no occasion. Pandora was seized with an eager curiosity to know what this jar contained; and one day she slipped off the cover and looked in. Forthwith there escaped a multitude of plagues for hapless man—such as gout, rheumatism, and colic for his body, and envy, spite, and revenge for his mind—and scattered themselves far and wide. Pandora hastened to replace the lid! but, alas! the whole contents of the jar had escaped, one thing only excepted, which lay at the bottom, and that was *hope*. So we see at this day, whatever evils are abroad, hope never entirely leaves us; and while we have *that*, no amount of other ills can make us completely wretched.

I think the story of Pandora is firmly linked with mirror visions. First she activates the jar by removing the lid, which is clearly reminiscent of the ritualistic acts required to prime the speculum. Then there are entities that emerge from the vessel when it is opened and after she looks into it. The Greek word for these entities is *keres*, little noisome and troublesome spirits. Their escape is reminiscent of the murderous genie in the bottle and the dragons that disturb the peace in Lludd's domain.

Pandora suffers the disapprobation the mirror gazer seems destined to receive, and she is clearly portrayed as the villain of the myth. The domestic disturbance brought about by her lid lifting is the central theme of the piece. Her disobedience brings widespread disarray in the world and is responsible for every kind of evil and sickness known to mankind.

There is an implied association with death in this story that would have been immediately grasped by readers in ancient times. That connection is the *pithos* jar itself, which was a very large container often used as a sort of coffin in which to bury paupers. The jar that belongs to Pandora's husband, Epimetheus, is in some way special, but exactly how is a mystery.

The link between the Pandora story and mirror gazing is even more strongly suggested by the existence of a ritual practiced in ancient Rome hundreds of years after the Pandora legend. It is so similar to gazing into a jar that I can't help thinking that there is a connection between the Greek myth and reality.

The ancient Romans had a round pit called the *mundus*. Normally the pit was covered by a large lid made of a precious blue stone that we now know as lapis. The pit was filled with liquid, most likely water or wine. On three days during the year—August 24, October 5, and November 6—the lid was removed in a ritual that was associated with ghosts.

The Roman historian Varro says that "when the *mundus* is open, the gate of the doleful underworld gods is open."

So, I believe, in my own way I have opened up Pandora's jar. Yet from this modern jar will surely spring good things, such as hope and understanding.

Scholars may find that mirror visions are the wellspring of many of our great myths and legends. I daresay that such a possibility has probably never presented itself to those who study the origins of these tales. But as I read ancient literature, I find more and more indications that mirror visions have influenced the stories that have contributed to civilizations.

Although there are many lines of research possible, my main interest lies in the clinical setting, where I can work closely with people seeking reunion with departed loved ones. It is there that the bold and puzzling experiences take place.

A woman who came for a visionary reunion with her son sums it up better than I can. Her son had died two years before she came to my psychomanteum. He died of cancer, which he had been fighting for several years. His battle against this disease had been typical of the many who fight it. The cancer would go into remission, and just as they thought that it had been beaten, it would come raging back again. Finally, after several relapses, he simply gave up.

The woman missed her son terribly. She came to the psychomanteum in hopes of seeing him one more time, just to see if the pain was gone.

We prepared all day for the encounter, and then I had her go into the apparition booth. The experience she had was satisfying. She saw a number of "memory visions," vivid snippets from his childhood. She also reported a strong sense that her son had been present with her in the booth. "He was sitting there with me," she said when she came out. "We sat there together and watched events from our life together."

A few days later I received an incredible call from her. A few days after her visit to my clinic, she awoke from a deep sleep. She didn't simply wake up, she became "hyperawake. Far more awake than normal."

There, standing in her room, was her son. As she sat up in bed to look at him, she could see that the ravages of cancer were gone. He now looked vibrant and happy as he had before his disease.

The woman was in a state of ecstasy. She stood up and faced her son and began carrying on a conversation. She estimates that they spoke for several minutes, time enough for her to find that he was now pain-free and happy.

They talked about a number of things, including the remodeling that the woman had done to the house after the son had died. She even took him on a tour of some of the rooms where changes had been made to show him what had been done.

Finally it dawned on her what was happening. She was talking to an apparition of her late son. "I couldn't believe it was him," she said to me. "So I asked if I could touch him."

Without a moment's hesitation this apparition of her son stepped forward and hugged her. Then, the woman said, he lifted her right off the ground and over his head.

"What happened was as real as if he had been standing right there," the woman told me. "I now feel as though I can put my son's death behind me and get on fully with my life."

Compelled by visions like that, I, too, press on.

BIBLIOGRAPHY

Ayer, Fred. *Before the Colors Fade*. Boston: Houghton Mifflin, 1964.

Barrett, Sir William. *Deathbed Visions: The Psychical Experiences of Dying*. The Colin Wilson Library of the Paranormal. Aquarian Press, 1986.

Belo, Jane. *Trance in Bali*. New York: Columbia University Press, 1960.

Bennett, E. *Apparitions and Haunted Houses*. London: Faber and Faber, 1939.

Besterman, Theodore. *Collected Papers on the Paranormal*. Garrett Publications, 1968.

—*Crystal Gazing: A Study in the History, Distribution, Theory and Practice of Scrying*. University Books, 1965.

Bulfinch, Thomas. *The Age of Fable or Beauties of Mythology*. New York: A Mentor Book, 1962.

Bulgatz, Joseph. *Ponzie Schemes, Invaders from Mars and More Extraordinary Popular Delusions and the Madness of the Crowds*. Harmony Books, 1992.

Burton, Richard F. (trans.) Adapted by Jack Zipes. *The Arabian Nights*. Penguin Books, 1991.

Day, Jane. *Aztec: The World of Moctezuma*. Denver:

Denver Museum of Natural History and Roberts Rinehart Publishers, 1992.

Deacon, Richard. *John Dee: Scientist, Geographer, Astrologer and Secret Agent to Elizabeth I.* The Garden City Press Limited, 1968.

Dee, Dr. John. *A True & Faithful Relation of What Passed for Many Years Between Dr. John Dee (A Mathematician of Great Fame in Queen Elizabeth and King James Their Reignes) and Some Spirits: etc.* Redwood Burn Limited, Trowbridge & Esher, 1974.

Dumas, François Ribadeau. Translated by Elisabeth Abbott. *Cagliostro.* George Allen and Unwin Ltd., 1966.

Edelstein, Emma J., and Ludwig Edelstein. *Asclepius: A Collection and Interpretation of the Testimonies, Vols. I and II.* Reprint Edition. Ayer Company Publishers, Inc., 1988.

Eliade, Mircea. *Shamanism: Archaic Techniques of Ecstasy.* Princeton, N.J.: Princeton University Press, 1964.

French, Peter. *John Dee: The World of an Elizabethan Magus.* Dorset Press, 1972.

Gauld, Alan. *The Founders of Psychical Research.* Routledge & Kegan Paul, 1968.

Goethe, Johann Wolfgang von. Translated by Abraham Hayward. *Faust by Goethe.* Hutchinson & Co. Publishers Ltd.

Goldberg, Benjamin. *The Mirror and Man.* University Press of Virginia, 1985.

Harrison, Jane Ellen. *Prolegomena to the Study of Greek Religion.* Princeton, N.J.: Princeton University Press, 1991.

Hastings, Arthur. "Psychomanteum Research: Experiences and Effects on Bereavement" in *Omega*. Vol 45. Edited by Kenneth Doka. Baywood Publishing, 2002.

Herodotus. Translated by Aubrey de Selincourt. *The Histories*. Penguin Books, 1972.

Homer. Translated by W H. D. Rouse. *The Odyssey*. A Mentor Book, New American Library, 1937.

Hultkrantz, Ake. Translated by Monica Setterwall. *The Religions of the American Indians*. University of California Press, 1967.

Jackson, Kenneth Hurlstone (trans.) *A Celtic Miscellany*. Penguin Books, 1951.

Kieckhefer, Richard. *Magic in the Middle Ages*. Cambridge, Eng.: Cambridge University Press, 1989.

King, Frank. *Cagliostro: The Last of the Sorcerers*. London: Jarrolds Publishers, 1929.

Lang, Andrew. *The Making of Religion*. AMS Press, 1968.

Leeds, Morton, and Gardner Murphy. *The Paranormal and the Normal: A Historical, Philosophical and Theoretical Perspective*. The Scarecrow Press, Inc., 1980.

Lindsay, Charles (photographs and journals), and Reimar Schefold (historical essay). *Mentawai Shaman: Keeper of the Rain Forest*. An Aperture Book, 1991.

Loewe, Michael, and Carmen Blacker *(eds.)*. *Divination and Oracles*. George Allen & Unwin, 1981.

MacKay, Charles. *Extraordinary Popular Delusions and the Madness of Crowds*. New York: Farrar Straus Giroux, 1932.

MacKenzie, Alexander. *The Prophecies of the Brahan Seer*.

Stirling: Eneas MacKay, 1909.

Mavromatitis, Andreas. *Hypnagogia: The Unique State of Consciousness Between Wakefulness and Sleep.* Routledge & Kegan Paul Ltd., 1987.

Mishlove, Jeffrey. *Thinking Allowed.* Council Oaks Books, 1992.

Morse, Melvin, M.D., with Paul Perry. *Transformed by the Light: The Powerful Effect of Near-Death Experiences on People's Lives.* New York: Villard Books, 1992.

Panofsky, Dora and Erwin. *Pandora's Box: The Changing Aspects of a Mythical Symbol.* Princeton, N.J.: Princeton University Press, 1991.

Parke, H. W. *Greek Oracles.* Hutchinson University Library, 1967.

Pausanias. Translated by Peter Levi. *Guide to Greece, Vols. I and II.* Penguin Glassies, 1971.

Plato. *The Republic* (B. Jowett, trans.). New York: Random House, 1955.

Rawcliffe, D. H. *Occult and Supernatural Phenomena.* Dover Publications, 1959.

Schultes, Richard Eyans, and Hoffman, Albert. *Plants of the Gods: Their Sacred, Healing and Hallucinogenic Powers.* Healing Arts Press, 1979.

Strabo. Translated by Horace Leonard Jones. *The Geography of Strabo, Vol. II* Cambridge, Mass.: Harvard University Press, Loeb Classical Library, 1917.

Thomas, Northcote W. *Crystal Gazing: Its History and Practice, with a Discussion of the Evidence for Telepathic Scrying.* Dodge Publishing Company, 1905; Health Research, 1968.

Toynbee, Arnold, *A Study of History*. London and New York: Oxford University Press, 1935–1961.

Trowbridge, W.R.H. *Cagliostro: Savant or Scoundrel? The True Role of This Splendid, Tragic Figure:* University Books (n.d.)

Vandenberg, Phillipp. *The Mystery of the Oracles.* Macmillan Publishing Company, Inc., 1979.

The Light Beyond

Raymond Moody

In his ground-breaking work, *Life After Life*, Dr Raymond Moody pioneered research into the 'near-death experience' or NDE. In this, his stunning sequel, he explores how many NDE survivors have uncannily similar stories to tell, and considers what their extraordinary stories can teach us.

As Dr Moody reveals, those who return from an NDE invariably talk of incredible out-of-body travel, of meeting heavenly beings or deceased loved ones, and of returning to consciousness with a greater appreciation of life. Dr Moody examines the moving experiences of children as well as adults, and shows how recent findings seem to confirm rather than refute their stories.

Engaging with expert witnesses from medicine, psychiatry and sociology, Dr Moody asks challenging questions and provides intriguing answers to those who wonder about dying. His message is provocative yet offers a reassuring glimpse of hope from the frontier between life and death.